Time Management for Teams

Merrill E. Douglass
and
Donna N. Douglass

American Management Association

New York • Atlanta • Boston • Chicago • Kansas City • San Francisco • Washington, D.C.
Brussels • Toronto • Mexico City

*This publication is designed to provide accurate and authoritative
information in regard to the subject matter covered. It is sold with
the understanding that the publisher is not engaged in rendering
legal, accounting, or other professional service. If legal advice or
other expert assistance is required, the services of a competent
professional person should be sought.*

Library of Congress Cataloging-in-Publication Data

Douglass, Merrill E.
      *Time management for teams / Merrill E. Douglass and Donna N.
  Douglass.*
        p.   cm.
      Includes bibliographical references and index.
      ISBN 0-8144-7804-2
      *1. Work groups—Time management.   I. Douglass, Donna N.
  II. Title.*
  HD66.D68   1992
  658.4'02—dc20   *92-22118*
                                                              CIP

Printing number

10   9   8   7   6   5   4   3   2   1

To
all
our
children

Contents

Preface and Acknowledgments

Since 1972, our work has been to help people make good use of their time. Our first book, *Manage Your Time, Manage Your Work, Manage Yourself* (1980), identified many of the problems and solutions as we saw them then. Can it really be so many years ago? Even though managing time is our daily focus, we're still surprised when it seems to pass so quickly. We simply can't resist the temptation to say, "Time sure flies when you're having fun!"

Naturally, we've changed over the years, and we've continued to learn more about good time management. That's the reason for this book: to share what we've been learning with our readers.

If you believe everything you see and hear, every company in the United States is in favor of teamwork. Some of this is only lip service, but some is sincere. More and more people are working in teams these days. This is a growing trend that will probably continue. However, the time management literature is universally targeted to individuals. We felt the need to say something about how teams can manage time well. That makes this a unique time management book.

There's another feature that makes this book unique. For the first time, we address the issue of temperament—personality style—and how it affects the use of time. No other time management book has ever explored this topic. However, we believe this information will provide valuable insights into team time issues. No doubt about it, we're all different, and we need to remember these individual differences when considering team time management.

Another major point we've learned is that good time

management involves positive relationships as well as productive results. There is a synergism between the two, and we need to keep them both in balance. There has been too much emphasis on results, often at the expense of relationships. Teams that hope to survive and thrive must be more sensitive to this balance. If nothing else, developing a keen competitive edge requires it.

Speaking of relationships, we want to express our deepest gratitude to the many, many people who have been part of our growth and development over the past twenty years. We realize, as never before, just how much we all need the contributions of others to keep growing.

First of all, a special thank-you goes to several people who have been particularly helpful on our journey into the temperaments. Our friend Florence Littauer first introduced us to the idea of temperaments many years ago, and her books *Personality Plus* (Old Tappan, N.J.: Fleming Revell, 1983) and *Your Personality Tree* (Waco, Tex.: Word Books, 1986) continue to be among our favorites. More recently, other friends such as Ken Voges and Ron Braund, authors of *Understanding How Others Misunderstand You* (Chicago: Moody Press, 1990), have provided many insights and helped us to think our way through the issues. Pat McMillan, of Team Resources, worked with us to refine our thoughts into something useful. Without these people, the issue of personal style could never have been such a unique feature of this book.

We hope you will enjoy reading this book as much as we have enjoyed writing it. Even more, we hope the information in this book will prove valuable to you.

May all your times be good times.

1
Why Team Time Management?

"Team time management? What for? I try to manage my time well; everyone else should do the same. If I do my job, and do it well, why in the world do I have to think in terms of teamwork?"

That's a fair question. Since the 1960s, we've all been urged to mange our time better. And we've all learned—some of us more reluctantly than others—to set goals and priorities, schedule our days, make a plan, and carry out that plan. Those of us who have worked our plans well have achieved a fair amount of success and are happy with the results. Why do we have to move beyond ourselves?

Time is a very personal issue. As the clock ticks away, day after day, so do our lives. Centuries ago, in agricultural societies, people paid little attention to managing their time; they simply took its passage for granted. They were born; they lived; they worked; they died. It was a simpler way of life, governed more by the changes in climate and seasons than by clocks. Although many maintain that this was a better time, there is no real proof that it was. It's just that it wasn't clock-driven.

After World War II, the pace began to pick up. Industrialization and technology called for more efficiency and the movement to more exact measurement of what was taking place. In one sense, this was when "time management" was born. Although Frank and Lillian Gilbreth did their revolutionary time and motion studies in the early twentieth century, their ideas were valued initially by only a small circle of visionaries. It wasn't until the 1940s and 1950s that the Gilbreths' ideas were absorbed into the mainstream of everyday thought. In the quest for greater profits, industrial engineering became an important part of improving productivity. Time was starting to move faster and become more demanding. The clock was beginning to tick louder in the minds of competitive Americans.

Today, as the twenty-first century hovers over the horizon, the idea of managing time is taking on a new, expanded meaning. Our concept of time must be larger; the clock itself must be bigger. Individual effort is no longer enough. Yes, it is still beneficial for individuals to strive for good personal time management skills. But this isn't enough. Just as a well-made brick does nothing when it stands alone, well-managed individuals have minimal usefulness until they are integrated into a synergistic whole. When the individual works together with others, the wall of effectiveness grows, adding to the greater productivity of everyone involved. Together we can do more than the total sum of our individual efforts.

It is always good to ask ourselves, "What's the best use of my time?" But the larger question to ask is, "What's the best use of *our* time?" No one works in a vacuum. No one gets much done alone. Top performance demands the joint efforts of many people working together toward a common goal. The greater concern is not just for personal time management but for team time management.

Increased competition from abroad and higher production costs at home have led to massive reorganizations, usually resulting in flatter and leaner organizations. Everyone must perform at peak levels if the company is to survive, let alone thrive. At the same time, there must be a less hierarchical approach to management, with each person becoming a vital key to success. Indeed, as the business climate grows more complex and demanding, the key to everyone's success lies more in team effort than in individual effort.

What About Rugged Individualism?

But what about the hallowed concept of the rugged individual? Historically, we have prospered and flourished as a nation when people "looked out for number one." The lone maverick, the individual against "the system," has long fascinated us and inspired our admiration. Can we reasonably ask people now to replace their focus on the individual with a focus on the group?

First, we're not arguing that individualism is bad, only that it needs to be balanced with teamwork. This balancing act is not easy, and sometimes requires subordinating personal interests to group interests. This is usually difficult, because most people think largely about themselves, even though many don't want to admit it. We focus on our goals, our problems, our work, our interests but spend very little time thinking about other people's goals, problems, work, or interests. Effective teamwork requires thinking about others much more often.

Second, more people than we might care to admit aren't really all that successful in getting ahead when they focus on themselves. Although many of us like to think we are self-sufficient, can-do-it-all people, most of us are actually very limited in what we can accomplish strictly on our own. Many of us are secretly frustrated by our inability to do it all ourselves. We feel like failures because, although we pretend to be strong individuals, we don't in fact feel that way.

> Just as a well-made brick does nothing when it stands alone, well-managed individuals have minimal usefulness until they are integrated into a synergistic whole.

It's true that each of us has certain talents and abilities, but there is generally at least one important element missing that will keep us from seeing an idea or a major goal to completion. We may say we value the individual, but we human beings are social creatures, meant to interact and work with each other, capitalizing on the strengths of each other and sharing our abilities where they are needed. While doing things on our own appeals to the private or selfish streak in our natures, our need for and dependence on others can be saving characteristics in more ways than one.

Finally, when people work together, they are far more than the sum of their parts. Their efforts form something much greater, granting each participant a share in something beyond their individual capacities.

At the signing of the Declaration of Independence in 1776, Benjamin Franklin said, "We must all hang together, or assuredly we shall all hang separately." Our forefathers hung together very well indeed, and achieved a remarkable success in the face of overwhelming challenges. Today we face new challenges, and teamwork can be a positive force for us, too, once we make that mental shift to a focus on group accomplishment.

The Golden Rule

There are other problems when we focus exclusively on our own goals, one of the biggest being the problems we create for those around us. Most of these problems are caused unintentionally, but they still hinder progress. We may delegate haphazardly as we attempt to check off items on our to-do lists. We often interrupt other people's train of thought by calling for their attention on the spur of the moment. Almost everyone identifies office chitchat as a waste of time, yet we feel entitled to tell our own stories whenever we feel the urge.

A more basic problem is that most of us have only a vague idea of what's going on around us. Some of us don't even know how our job fits in with that of the person sitting next to us. A focus on teamwork is a big step toward alleviating the problem of internal interruptions in the office. Once we know what our co-workers are doing, we have greater respect for their time.

The Golden Rule is an ancient admonition to dust off and

use regularly. It provides a strong foundation for effective teamwork. Every advanced culture for thousands of years has recommended this. Think about it carefully: Treat others the way you would like them to treat you. It's really that simple—and really that difficult as well. It is much more than a syrupy platitude. It is absolutely sound business advice. If we all did this regularly, miracles would take place. The results would be tremendous.

Us–vs.–Them Thinking

Another problem with promoting individualism is that many of us believe we're okay; it's the other guy who's the problem. A great deal of "themism" is making the rounds today. We see it in all areas of life. Political surveys show that the majority of Americans believe elected legislators are scalawags and scoundrels—except their own representatives, who are okay. So we keep reelecting the incumbents, and complaining about the problems they create in Washington. Surveys also show that most people agree that U.S. schools are in deep trouble. However, they feel that the schools in their own community are doing a good job. Very few people disagree with the teaching of the Golden Rule. It's just that they think it is other people who should make a greater effort to apply it, because, after all, they are already doing a pretty good job themselves!

Yes, our organizations would improve if only "they" would improve. The referent *they* might mean subordinates, peers, management, suppliers, government, or even things in general. Passing the blame off on "them" relieves us of the responsibility for changing. If we're not doing an excellent job, at least we're doing as well as anyone else.

No doubt, others do create problems. But there is also a bigger danger. So long as you focus on some outside force as the source of your problem, you never see the total picture. You actually begin to believe in your own immunity and non-responsibility. When top management engages in this kind of fuzzy thinking, the results are especially disastrous.

Efforts to change others by telling them the "right" way to do things are usually a waste of time and may even cause more problems. There is a natural resistance to being told what to do, and it has nothing to do with the time teamwork we're advocating. Time teamwork focuses on a team effort, not on dictatorial leadership.

What Is Meant by Team Time Management?

Team time management requires an entirely new approach to time management. It suggests that the tempo of the organization is focused on groups of people working together, not on individuals. It requires that we learn to think and act with respect to our time as it fits into the bigger picture. This is not to diminish the individual, but to enlarge the individual's perception.

A team approach to time management has many advantages that usually go unnoticed. First, team time management aims to use everyone's time to best advantage. In a team effort, there is a greater abundance of the skills and abilities needed for handling the job. This increases the likelihood that a person with an aptitude for a particular activity will be the one selected to do it. A person who likes a task usually does it better and faster than a person who dislikes it.

With a team approach to time, a large number of similar activities can be grouped together and executed by fewer people. This saves learning time, start-up time, and wind-down time as well.

Most of all, with a team approach, time can readily be viewed as the valuable resource it truly is. When a number of people are involved and accountable to one another, the results are almost always better.

The pivotal position for developing team time management is that of the manager or team leader. The manager has the potential to make team time management an exciting improvement. The manager also has the potential to completely undermine the entire system.

Some managers have fought hard to become "the boss." They like bossing. Depending on their personality type, many enjoy giving orders, seeing their ideas put in action, and controlling the work of others. Most of their thoughts of what it means to be a manager were formed under the old hierarchical management system. This approach has changed very little since Frederick Taylor's scientific management of the early 1900s: The boss makes the decisions and the workers do what they are told.

In all the years we've been doing time management training, the boss has often been identified as a time problem. In our most recent survey, comments like this were frequently made:

> "He assigns me projects when he really doesn't know exactly what he wants."
>
> "She blames me for mistakes that are really her fault."
>
> "My boss always expects me to drop whatever I'm doing to cater to his latest whim. He never thinks about the problem this causes me."

Of course, people are more inclined to express these thoughts when their boss isn't around. There is also a tendency for some people to misinterpret and blame the boss for everything, whether it is deserved or not. And, yes, there is always the other side of the argument—the boss is not the only culprit. However, we believe that many of the time management problems we've seen over the years have been caused by poor supervision. Many managers express the attitude that their agenda—and their time—is more important than anyone else's. This alone accounts for thousands of hours of frustration and lost productivity. It certainly fails to foster a team spirit. Many bosses refuse to accept this criticism. Their refusal means that the problem will continue. Once the boss accepts the fact that he or she may be the problem, improvement becomes much easier.

Enter a New Kind of Manager

An American Management Association publication recently declared that "the autocratic manager—'the boss'—comfortably housed in a paternalistic organization will soon be a relic of the past. The new order will see much more give-and-take between managers and staffers."* The end of "the boss" is near; it can't come too soon. For too long we've had far more managers than we needed, and they have created far too many problems.

Why move to team time management? The most compelling reason is that the old model no longer works. Gone are the days when a "satisfactory" performance was good enough to get ahead on. Competition no longer allows it. It is good business sense to work with a team concept. Managers who want to succeed must be open to making the changes required.

In the future, we will see flatter organizations, more self-directed work teams, and more knowledgeable workers. Different patterns of work, like flexible hours, job sharing, or working at home via computers, will probably increase. As organizations and work structures change, so will the role of the manager.

Management style must be matched to new conditions. If not, managers will create tremendous time problems. We see at least four fundamental changes that must occur in the role of managers:

1. *The manager as more of a servant, less of a boss.* It's time to tip the pyramid upside down. Frederick Taylor's dictum that "managers think and plan, and workers do what they are told" will no longer work. Relying on formal authority structures is increasingly dysfunctional. Those who manage best understand that it is more important to serve than to be served. This will be a drastic change in the way many managers think.

2. *The manager as more of a coach, less of a controller.* The old model assumed that managers knew best. Much energy was spent keeping employees in line. The new model requires unlocking the creative potential of all workers. This means seeing workers in a new light. Some say that this switch from directing to influencing will be the biggest paradigm shift of all.†

*Human Resources Forum Newsletter, American Management Association, February 1992.
†Beverly Beber, "From Manager Into Coach," *Training*, February 1992.

3. *The manager as more of a facilitator, less of a roadblock.* Peter Drucker once said, "Much of what we call management consists of making it difficult for people to work."* Recently, Drucker has indicated that many of the rules and regulations that hamper productivity stem more from management paranoia than from real reasons.† The key rationale for having managers is to make it easier for people to achieve greater results in less time, to get more done with managers than they could without managers.

4. *The manager as someone who empowers people, not depowers them.* Managers will delegate even more authority to lower levels. They will be master motivators, creating an environment in which people can flourish and grow. This means more trust on both sides. When that happens, everyone will get more done in less time.

Empowering people is not easy for managers who were trained under the old system and who basically do not trust workers. Nevertheless, people tend to rise or fall to meet our expectations. Expect the best from staff members, and you will usually get it. Treat them as trustworthy, and they will be. Show them respect and boost their sense of self-worth, and watch them soar.

To foster good team time management we must examine, and probably change, many policies and practices. We should scrap many of the status symbols that separate us and create ill-will. We should abolish productivity cripplers like job descriptions and performance appraisals. We must earnestly work at developing a "we" attitude and of making our words and our actions consistent.

Fear of Change

We have discussed the idea of team time management with a number of professionals and support staff from many different

*Personal conversation.

†"The Nonprofit Drucker," audiocassettes (Tyler, Tex.: Leadership Network, 1989).

industries. They have shared their thoughts openly with us. For many, there is some hesitation in moving away from an individual emphasis toward a team approach. One person pointed out that, "Our organization is in the middle of cut-backs. Everyone is very 'turf' conscious at the moment, so this wouldn't work." Many people are, indeed, fearful of losing their jobs. They are thinking about survival, not improving productivity. This is especially true among mid-level managers as companies delete multiple layers of management.

Probably the greatest concern expressed to us, however, had to do with changing old habits and work patterns. "I'm used to my old ways." "Some people just don't like to change." "People around here will never change." What people are accustomed to is the biggest stumbling block to any change. We don't want to go through the discomfort of changing even if the change might make things better. We're so comfortable with our old discomforts that we prefer to keep them rather than risk an alternative.

Why do people resist change? Let's look at this question for just a moment, because the answer holds an important key. The following list contains many of the reasons people give for resisting change:

- We have no input into changes.
- We remember negative experiences from past changes.
- The changes threaten our jobs.
- The change reduces our job satisfaction.
- There is poor communication about the change.
- The timing of the change is bad.
- The change means more work for us.
- We don't see the need for the change.
- The change disrupts our work habits.
- We see the change as personal criticism.
- We don't trust management.

Contrary to what many believe, people can actually enjoy and welcome change. It all depends on how the change is handled. Unfortunately, much of the change in organizations is handled very poorly.

Change is inevitable. It occurs whether or not you like it or want it. Therefore, it is better to do your best to plan for the changes and to try to handle them well. The worst thing you can do is to wait until the change is forced upon you. Be proactive.

Team time management has the potential to answer many problems. It provides a win-win model and has few drawbacks. However, it takes vision, courage, and maturity.

Be willing to take a chance. Discover the greater potential that lies within the group. Why? Not simply because these ideas sound good, but because our economic future depends on it.

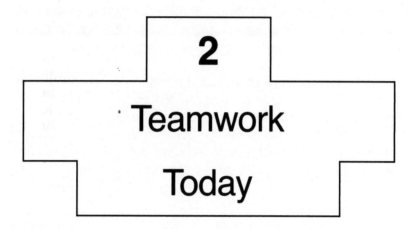

2

Teamwork

Today

What comes to mind when you hear the word *team*? The first image many of us see is an athletic team. Certainly when we were young that's what a team was. If you were on a baseball team, a football team, a tennis team, or even a debating team, you were taught that to win the game it was more important to work together than to work separately. In fact, players who focused totally on themselves and tried to become a one-man show soon discovered they were "on the bench." The team failed if the individual players didn't work for the good of all.

Business teams are still too new for many of us to have a common feeling about what is meant by teamwork. We'll have a fair amount of success, however, if we simply transpose the athletic model from the playground to the sleek, fluorescent-lit offices we find ourselves in today. Teamwork was easy to understand on the playground; it's mandatory that we also understand it in the office.

Webster defines a team as a "group working together." However, we must dig a little deeper in search of understanding. By adding a few more useful, telling words, we find that *team* also means "collections of people who must rely on group collaboration if each member is to experience the optimum of success and goal achievement." This definition suggests a whole lot more than the first definition, promoting the inter-dependency of group members and emphasizing the goal of optimum success for all concerned.

Teams can be large or small, but frequently consist of management groups, committees, task forces, self-directed work teams, and other work units that strive to act as one. The team goal is the focus, much as the goalpost is in a football game or the basket in a basketball game. Each team member does whatever it takes for the team to score.

Group vs. Team

Many people think that a group and a team are the same thing. We don't wish to belabor the point, but we do need to differ-entiate between the two in some way. Teamwork is far more demanding and far more rewarding than the group work most of us recall. The differences between being part of a group and being part of a team are important ones.

Most of us already work in some kind of group in which we are dependent on others to some degree. Sometimes, however, these groups are simply collections of people pulled together for administrative purposes only. Members still work more independently than dependently and are sometimes even at cross purposes with each other. Rather than participating in the decision-making process, members are often told what to do. Game playing and conflict are common, though not always resolved. Conformity is often more important than results.

Exceptional performance requires more teamwork than most groups exhibit. Teams require more commitment and involvement. In teams, people are interdependent, jointly own team goals, and work together more cooperatively. Participa-tion is mandatory, and individual uniqueness is accepted. Results, rather than conformity, are paramount. Teamwork is cooperation at its best. This is perhaps what Tom Peters meant when he said that greater competition requires greater cooper-ation.*

*Tom Peters, "Winds of Change Buffet Central Staffs," *Executive Edge* news-letter (January 1992), p. 3.

Teams generally exhibit more trust among members than do groups. Team members stick together and look out for each other. Managers of groups are more likely to go along with upper management than they are to look out for the best interests of the group and may even view other members as threatening.

In teams, problem solving is a central responsibility of the team in which everyone is expected to participate. In groups, solving a problem together is often considered a waste of time by the people involved and perhaps an abdication of personal responsibility.

One of the most negative effects of a group approach is that conflict between staff members is often swept under the carpet or ignored altogether. As a result, conflict is allowed to fester until it becomes nearly unmanageable. It can even reach the point where individual survival becomes more important than the original achievement goal.

In a well-organized team, there is a conscious effort to mediate conflicts before they become destructive. There is a basic recognition of individual differences and perspectives as a potential source of conflict. Paying attention to these differences can help avoid many pitfalls.

In a group focus, communication is often controlled and tight. Information may be limited on a "need to know" basis. In a team approach, communication flows freely. Questions and ideas are encouraged. Members of the team are permitted to reach their own conclusions and encouraged to provide their unique input into the decision-making process.

Team leaders, of course, have a totally different style than those content to be group managers. Team leaders must have a confidence level and maturity level far exceeding the demands of the old management style. Teams require leaders who possess all the characteristics of the "new managers" described in Chapter 1. Groups too often suffer under "the boss."

In short, teams exhibit more of a Theory Y orientation to work and people, whereas many groups are still based on the Theory X belief structure.

Theory X	Theory Y
1. Work is inherently distasteful to most people.	1. Work is as natural as play if the conditions are favorable.
2. Most people are lazy and irresponsible.	2. People want to work and will accept responsibility.
3. Most people have little capacity for creativity in solving problems.	3. The capacity for creativity in solving problems is widely distributed in the population.
4. People must be motivated externally.	4. People are motivated internally.
5. Most people must be closely controlled and often coerced to achieve work goals.	5. People can be self-directed and will work hard to achieve goals if properly motivated.

Characteristics of Effective Teams

What exactly does an effective team look like? Here are several characteristics of successful teams that can serve as goals for anyone hoping to develop a team approach. Adjustments, of course, may be necessary to fit the specific needs of various organizations, but the following ideals should be held in high esteem:

1. *Goals.* Goals are the first step. Each person on the team must understand and share in the team goals and be dedicated to their achievement. Goals are important even for people working individually, but when they work with others they are essential. Common, shared goals permit the development of a "single-minded" team.

2. *Expression.* Each team member is entitled to free expression. Each member is also entitled to an audience that listens and responds empathetically. In fact, membership on a team carries with it the obligation to listen to other team members. This ensures that all sides of an issue are covered and increases the possibilities for achieving positive results.

3. *Leadership.* Each team member must be willing to take a leadership role as necessary. Through an understanding of individual strengths and weaknesses, each person will feel free to volunteer to meet the various needs of the team. The same person will not always be the leader.

4. *Consensus.* A team consensus is sought and also tested. The team strives to reach the best conclusions without unduly pressuring individual members into agreement.

5. *Trust.* Team members trust one another. They feel comfortable telling other team members information they would be hesitant to share with those outside the team. They also feel free to express a counter viewpoint without fearing that they will suffer negative consequences for being out of step.

6. *Flexibility.* The team constantly seeks new and better ways to perform. Members realize that time and circumstances will change both the team as a whole and themselves as individuals. The team actively looks for better ways to work together and to help members find improved methods.

These six points should be reviewed often by any team organizer or team member who is involved either in forming a team or in continuing a team that has already been developed. You may want to enlarge this list to include characteristics gained from your own experiences. Use these points as a guide and mirror. These characteristics require much work; they are not accomplished easily. But the closer a team gets to these ideals, the greater its chance of achieving its true potential.

> Keep slugging. Keep practicing team techniques.
> Inevitably, everyone will be a winner.

Overcoming the Barriers to Teamwork

Teamwork, at least in theory, should proceed smoothly and comfortably. There are multiple advantages, and even though many people are more accustomed to working individually, the potential payoffs of good teamwork make it an attractive alternative. Unfortunately, developing teamwork often turns out to be more difficult than it should be. Barriers crop up all over the place. Some of these barriers stem from personality conflicts between team members, an issue we cover in the next few chapters.

Other barriers, however, are just as important. Robert Lefton, president of Psychological Associates in St. Louis, has identified eight important problems that can sabotage team efforts.* Review the barriers carefully to see if they pose a problem in your organization.

1. *Breakdown in probing.* This refers to the ability to elicit information, the ability to dig deeper and to ask the right questions. If a manager or team leader lacks the ability to get to the heart of a problem or goal, he or she will fail to get accurate information—and the team effort will falter. Complete and accurate information is rarely presented spontaneously.

2. *Promotional leadership.* The promotional leader lets his or her position become known before everyone else has had a chance to express an opinion. For example, the leader may say, "I think we should take the XYZ bid; but, of course, I'd like to hear your opinions before I make a final decision." This sort of statement tends to stifle a free exchange of ideas, particularly among reticent people. A leader who is truly interested in hearing the ideas of all team members will refrain from expressing a personal opinion until after everyone has had an opportunity to speak freely.

3. *Intrateam conflict.* Conflict within a team is normal. In many ways, it's the life of a team. Team members frequently argue, debate, and "tell it like it is." That's healthy. The real problems occur when one or more members of the team sacrifice the team objectives for their own personal agendas. Synergism is lost, and all team efforts begin to crumble.

4. *Insufficient alternatives.* This can be a pitfall if the team

*Robert R. Lefton, "The Eight Barriers to Teamwork," *Personnel Journal,* January 1988.

or its leader gets "trigger happy" and wants to move into action too quickly. When this happens, the team fails to solicit all possible options from its members. It doesn't want to take the time to listen to all the "crazy" ideas. But remember, there is more danger in cutting off the brainstorming too early than there is in having too many ideas to choose from.

5. *Lack of candor.* Candor means full and accurate disclosure. A team will fail if its members aren't consistently candid. When candor is sacrificed, it's usually for one of two reasons: (1) People are afraid of hurting someone's feelings; or (2) intrateam politics makes it safer to keep one's mouth shut. When this happens, it works to the detriment of the team.

6. *Pointless meetings.* Meetings are called without having an objective or any real purpose. People get disgusted with pointless meetings because they waste time and produce nothing. All team meetings should have well-defined goals. We'll say much more about this in Chapter 8.

7. *Lack of self-critique.* Every team needs to examine itself regularly. It must "grade" itself. The best way to make sure this happens is to build a self-critique into the routine so that it can't easily be avoided.

8. *Failure to cycle downward.* Once the team has reached important conclusions, it must make its decisions known to all who will be affected by them. It those people whose collaboration is required don't know what's supposed to happen, nothing will.

Consider these eight points as warning signals. Review each one as it relates to your team efforts. No one said teamwork was easy, but we are continually learning more about how to make it successful. Smart teams learn from their own experiences as well as from those of others.

Some Selfish Reasons for Teamwork

An individual has much to gain when working successfully on a team. When a potential team member asks, "What's in it for me?" the honest answer is, "A lot!" A team member has clear priorities and goals that are understood by all teammates. In a team, a person is free to openly communicate because this is encouraged and required. In a team, conflict is normal and viewed as an opportunity. Resolution of the conflict is sure to follow, as productive procedures are established and followed. Finally, learning to work effectively as a team in one unit has transfer potential for other situations. Being a productive member of a team is a skill worth having. As teams become more and more valued, this skill will become even more important.

Remember, total success isn't built in a day. Trust will grow as the team works, overcomes obstacles, and finally discovers success. Members will learn to forgive each other for any perceived transgressions and move on to achieving results and stated goals. As in the days of our youth, team members will learn to support each other in the play and, home run after home run, eventually win the game. With enough practice, the team may even win a World Series now and then. The point is: Don't give up on your team. Keep slugging. Keep practicing team techniques. Inevitably, everyone will be a winner.

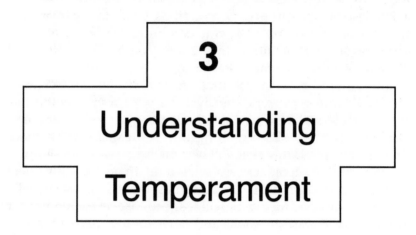

3

Understanding

Temperament

Would teamwork be easier if we were all alike? It's tempting to think so. After years of putting up with all kinds of people, it's fun to daydream about what it would be like if everyone thought like us, worked like us, understood like us. Some people would call such a work environment heaven; others might not be so sure. Would it really be better? What might be missing?

In the real world, of course, we are not all alike. Even those of us who think we're somewhat alike quickly find that there are many differences. There are even many different ways of interpreting the same event. Because of all these varying personalities, many of us would just as soon forget about the team idea and concentrate on doing our own thing.

Other people can, indeed, be frustrating. They may or may not be dependable. They talk at the wrong times about the wrong things, or they may not talk at all when they should. They like to interrupt, but they don't like to be interrupted. They hurt our feelings, and we hurt theirs; yet neither of us can understand why. It's definitely easier to stay in our own little world and ignore everyone else.

Of course, those who prefer to stay in their own little

world are some of the most difficult people to work with on a team. If you see yourself as one of these people, please stay with us. We need your valuable input in order to achieve the team goals. The talents you have, once you learn to share them, will enhance results for everyone. Stay tuned in.

Yes, it's good that we aren't all alike. The richness and diversity in different people is a big reason that teamwork can accomplish so much more. The challenge, of course, is overcoming the negative parts of each personality. It's these negative components grating against each other—that we call personality conflicts—that cause so many problems. On the other hand, the positive components, the talents and abilities of each personality, when blended together into a harmonious whole, can achieve results no one even imagined. We want to accentuate the positive and learn to overcome the negative.

Understanding individual differences is the first step—perhaps the most important—in moving beyond irritations and confusion to building effective teams. Once we develop the understanding we need, we can take these differences for what they are: unique personality traits. Once we can accept these traits, we can put them in proper perspective and move on to the talents and value of the person.

Understanding won't change people, but understanding can change the way people affect you. With understanding, you can control your irritation and move on. Remember, there are also many irritating things about you that others must overlook to appreciate your real value.

The Temperament Model

Psychologists have long argued about whether human behavior results from nature or nurture. Are we the way we are because we were born that way or because of the environment we grew up in? We believe it is both. Your basic temperament is set at birth; it is God's gift to you. Environmental conditioning helps determine how you will express your temperament. Personality is how you present yourself to others. It may or may not match your temperament. Personality is sometimes a mask, which can be stripped away under particularly trying or diffi-cult circumstances. What's underneath can surprise the indi-vidual, as well as others.

Each person is a unique blend of characteristics. No one else is exactly like you. We all see, think, act, and respond differently. We each approach time in our own individual way. No theory can ever fully explain everything about us, but a good theory can increase our understanding. Our goal in this chapter is to increase your understanding and awareness of the differences between yourself and others.

Although we know that people are different, we are slow to accept or tolerate these differences. Many of us assume that if everyone were okay, they'd be pretty much like we are. The unspoken assumption is that if you're different, you must be wrong. However, different does not mean wrong; different only means different. To better understand these differences, we must drop the idea of right and wrong. Such terms serve only to confuse the issue.

One of the most useful tools for understanding ourselves and others is the concept of temperament. Almost all person-ality theory has been based on four primary dimensions, or temperaments. This has been true for over 2,000 years. The ancient Greeks believed that body fluids were the source of these temperaments. Around 400 B.C., Hippocrates, the father of medicine, called the four temperaments choleric, sanguine, phlegmatic, and melancholy. The Chinese, around 700 A.D., labeled them after animals: elephants, butterflies, turtles, and beavers.

Not until the mid-twentieth century, however, did the theory become so well developed that ordinary people could benefit from it. Much of the credit belongs to Dr. William Marston, a Columbia University psychologist who also identi-fied four basic behavioral types by grouping people together according to the similarities in their ways of acting and react-ing.* Dr. Marston's identification scheme provided the tools that have become so useful in understanding the tempera-

---

*William Marston, *Emotions of Normal People* (Minneapolis, Minn.: Persona Press, 1979); originally published by Harcourt Brace in 1928.

ments. Most of the current temperament instruments based on Dr. Marston's work classify the temperaments as D, I, S, and C, standing for Dominance or Directness, Inducement or Influencing, Submission or Steadiness, and Compliance or Cautiousness.

Identifying Your Temperament

All the people in your work group have their own impressions of themselves and others, and these impressions probably have some validity. They are, however, usually inexact and incomplete. Furthermore, impressions provide no objective basis that individuals can share with one another. It is for this reason that temperament instruments are helpful.

The approach we're using here is a simple but effective one. All members of the team should participate whether or not they have any previous knowledge of the temperaments. It will provide a common basis for all involved and draw each person into the understanding process.

Read each of the following twelve sets of descriptive statements. There are four statements in each set. Select the *one* statement that most closely describes you.

1. _____ a. Adapt easily to others
   _____ b. Want my own way
   _____ c. Am fussy about my things
   _____ d. Like to have fun

2. _____ a. Am always analyzing things
   _____ b. Am generally undisciplined
   _____ c. Am fearful about what may happen
   _____ d. Get impatient with delays

3. _____ a. Face the future optimistically
   _____ b. Enjoy an orderly life
   _____ c. Have a forceful personality
   _____ d. Am generally satisfied with life

4. _____ a. Find things are usually in a haphazard
           condition
   _____ b. Am not very affectionate
   _____ c. Am generally very hard to please
   _____ d. Am timid and don't get involved much

5. _____ a. Am decisive and action-oriented
   _____ b. Am considerate and respectful
   _____ c. Am demonstrative and animated
   _____ d. Have a sense of humor

6. _____ a. Am a perfectionist in most things
   _____ b. Frequently talk too much
   _____ c. Tend to be intolerant
   _____ d. Am indifferent to many situations

7. _____ a. Like being the center of attention
   _____ b. Enjoy being in charge
   _____ c. Am a diplomatic peacemaker
   _____ d. Am critical of many situations

8. _____ a. Am thoughtful and logical
   _____ b. Am often late
   _____ c. Like to take it easy
   _____ d. Have a temper that flares easily

9. _____ a. Am cooperative and like to oblige friends
           and family
   _____ b. Get moody frequently
   _____ c. Enjoy being self-reliant
   _____ d. Like living spontaneously

10. _____ a. Keep careful records
    _____ b. Want credit for what I achieve
    _____ c. Am often in doubt about what to do
    _____ d. Am strongly competitive

11. _____ a. Produce a lot of work
    _____ b. Listen patiently to others
    _____ c. Am usually cheerful and lively
    _____ d. Am often pessimistic

12. _____ a. Tend to overlook details or to forget things
    _____ b. Am slow to get moving
    _____ c. Am stubborn in my opinions
    _____ d. Plan to organize things well

You should now have selected twelve statements that are most descriptive of you, one from each of the twelve sets of statements. The next step is to calculate your probable temperament. To do this, look at the scoring matrix in Figure 3-1. For

Figure 3-1. Scoring matrix for twelve sets of personality characteristics.

Statement Sets	Time Taskmaster	Time Teaser	Time Tarrier	Time Tender
1	b	d	a	c
2	d	b	c	a
3	c	a	d	b
4	b	a	d	c
5	a	c	d	b
6	c	b	d	a
7	b	a	c	d
8	d	b	c	a
9	c	d	a	b
10	d	b	c	a
11	a	c	b	d
12	c	a	b	d
Total				

each set of statements, place a check mark in the box that indicates the response you selected. For example, if you selected statement (b) in the first set of statements, then you would check the box where (b) appears on line in the matrix.

Total the number of check marks in each column. The higher your score in a column, the more of that temperament you have in your makeup. The column with the most checkmarks is your probable primary temperament. Our labels appear at the top of each column.

Before discussing each temperament in greater detail, it is important to note that each person is a blend of all four temperaments. No one is 100 percent any one temperament. For example, to say that you are a Time Taskmaster simply means that there is more of that dimension in your makeup than there is of other dimensions. However, you will also have some degree of the other three as well, and the four factors combine to make up your total behavioral style.*

As we've already indicated, many people over the years have labeled the temperaments differently. Each writer likes to add his or her own touch to the subject. The chart at the top of page 27 shows a comparison of some of the more common labels used today. No matter what labels you run across, you should have no trouble relating them to the descriptions provided in this chapter.

Each temperament has a different drive, or intent, that is meaningful in both individual and team settings. Time Taskmasters strive to overcome, to conquer, to dominate, to achieve results, to get things done. Time Teasers try to influence, express, persuade, and have fun. Time Tarriers strive to be steady and systematic, to be supportive and maintain harmony, to take it easy. Time Tenders strive to be accurate, sure,

*Many readers may want more information about temperament than can be provided in this chapter. The best way to discover details about your own temperament pattern is to use an instrument that measures the four factors. The best one we know of is the Personal DISCernment Inventory produced by Team Resources, Inc., 5500 Interstate North Parkway, Suite 425, Atlanta, Georgia 30328; tel. (404) 956–0985. This is an easy-to-use instrument—self-administered, self-scored, and self-interpreted—that in minutes reveals your personal temperament combination, measures the intensity of all four factors, and gives a detailed description of composite behavioral styles.

OUR LABEL	Time Taskmaster	Time Teaser	Time Tarrier	Time Tender
	Choleric	Sanguine	Phlegmatic	Melancholy
	Elephant	Butterfly	Turtle	Beaver
	D-Dominance	I-Influencing	S-Steadiness	C-Compliance
	Director	Socializer	Relater	Thinker
	Driving	Expressive	Amiable	Analytical
	Self-Reliant	Expressive	Loyal	Factual
	Achievers	Talkers	Accommodators	Thinkers
	Impulsive	Talkative	Timid	Deliberative

and safe, to avoid trouble and to do it right. Time Taskmasters and Time Tenders tend to be more task-oriented, whereas Time Teasers and Time Tarriers are more relationship-oriented. You can easily see the implications of these different temperament patterns for effective teamwork.

Understanding Dominant Time Taskmasters

Time Taskmasters are born leaders. They are take-charge people, whether they're two years old or fifty-two. They are frequently "the boss" because they seek supervisory positions. Even if they are not in charge, they often take charge anyway. They thrive on opposition and love to solve problems. They're self-starters, direct, positive, and straightforward. That's their nice side. They are also too blunt for their own good and are often organizational troublemakers. As they single-mindedly pursue the goal, they often hurt the feelings of others without even realizing it. They flare up quickly and just as quickly cool down again.

They will fight hard for what they believe is right, but can accept momentary defeat without holding grudges. They often hate routine and are prone to changing jobs, especially early in their careers. They thrive on competition, tough assignments, heavy work loads, pressure, and any opportunity for achievement. They demand a great deal of themselves and others. Their energy level is high, and they can exercise strong willpower when it helps them to reach their goals.

Time Taskmasters attack time to conquer it, trying to make the most of every minute. They usually arrive at appointments on time, but reserve the right to be late if something more important comes up. However, they don't like to wait for others, so they expect everyone else to be on time and wait for them, if necessary. From a time standpoint, they are easy on themselves but hard on others.

Their time management strengths include providing direction, setting goals, achieving results, deciding quickly, setting the pace, being proactive, accepting challenges, and stimulating activity. Their time management weaknesses include interrupting others often, overcommitting, being in a hurry, ignoring the system, not planning enough, being workaholic, demanding too much, and being pushy and overbearing.

Time Taskmasters feel secure when they are in control, and much of their behavior is directed to staying in control. They like to see results from their efforts. They create change to gain control. They measure personal worth by results, track record, and measurable progress. They are irritated by inefficiency and indecision. Under pressure, Time Taskmasters become bossy, impatient, blunt, sarcastic, and critical.

**Different does not mean wrong;
different only means different.**

Understanding Interacting Time Teasers

Time Teasers usually have a pleasing personality and a good sense of humor. They persuade where the Time Taskmaster coerces. People seem to respond naturally to them, and they make friends easily. They are innately optimistic and their natural people skills help them to get along with almost anyone, including their competitors. They enjoy interacting with other people and can't stand being cooped up by themselves. They love prestige, recognition, and being center-stage. They are expressive, confident, poised, and friendly.

They thrive on social contact, one-on-one situations, and

freedom from controls or details. They are spontaneous, loosely disciplined, and dislike structure. They can handle ambiguity well and enjoy change and variety. They're inspirational, creative, helpful, and articulate. They are usually energetic, although they often dissipate their energy by going in too many directions at the same time. If left to their own devices, Time Teasers may turn the team into a social club, and although it may be fun, very little work will get done. They are easily bored by details and often fail to follow through on things as they should.

Time Teasers tend to operate in the present. They don't like to pay too much attention to time, because time imposes structure. As a result, they are often late, but they are also tolerant when others are tardy. To a Time Teaser, relationships are more important than promptness. From a time standpoint, they are easy on themselves and easy on others, too.

Their time management strengths include volunteering for jobs, getting others involved, generating new ideas, helping and inspiring others, and adjusting quickly to change. Their time management weaknesses include frequent interruptions, inadequate planning, winging it too often, ignoring details, socializing too much, and not controlling time.

Time Teasers feel secure when they receive lots of positive encouragement and praise from others. They will go to great lengths to gain approval from those who are important to them. They promote change because it provides variety. They measure personal worth by recognition, applause, and compliments. They are irritated by boredom, routine, and structure. Under pressure, Time Teasers become impulsive, emotional, inconsistent, superficial, and unrealistic.

Understanding Supportive Time Tarriers

Time Tarriers are steady, amiable, relaxed, easygoing people. They identify strongly with groups and do not usually seek the spotlight for themselves. They probably adapt best to the ideas of time teamwork. They are practical, factual, and low-key. They don't pretend to be something they are not; what you see is what you get. They are generally content with the status quo and are slow to change. They resist pressure and attempt to avoid conflict.

They thrive in a relaxed, supportive atmosphere where they receive lots of affirmation. They prefer situations that offer security, limited territory, and predictable work routines. They do best when they feel appreciated. They are very oriented to personal relationships and seek to maintain harmony with others. They are often the glue that holds a group together. They are systematic, dependable, and patient. However, they can also be rather unexciting, unenthusiastic, slow, and stubborn.

Time Tarriers usually see time as a friend when they're not under pressure, but as an enemy when they're operating under imposed deadlines. As pressure builds, their performance slows down. They may arrive early or late, depending on what they have to do, but they are generally on time when they're in charge. They are forgiving when others are tardy. From a time standpoint, they tend to be hard on themselves but easy on others.

Their time management strengths include developing and maintaining systems, finding easier ways, being team-oriented, mediating problems, being good administrators, and handling logistics and details well. Their time management weaknesses include procrastinating, being slow starters, not setting goals, being slow workers, resisting change, and showing low initiative.

Time Tarriers feel secure when everything is in harmony and when they have lots of positive feedback from others. They value security at work and at home more than most. They resist change because it upsets stable relationships and harmony. They measure their own personal worth by the depth of their relationships and compatibility with others. They are irritated by insensitivity and impatience. Under pressure, Time Tarriers become sulky, stubborn, and unimaginative; they also hold grudges and procrastinate.

Understanding Competent Time Tenders

Time Tenders are precise, analytical, orderly, and cautious. They are attentive to details and make excellent planners, although they tend to get bogged down in analysis. Their tendency to pessimism helps them and others avoid potential problems. They hold to tradition and precedence and are slow to change. They are good at organizing almost anything, but are apt to prefer working alone to working as part of a team.

They thrive in orderly, conflict-free situations. They prefer a controlled work environment with the opportunity to produce high-quality, accurate work. They enjoy exact job descriptions and dislike sudden surprises. They tend to set idealistic or unrealistic goals, and feel overwhelmed about areas in which they don't measure up. Many have low energy levels and often get buried in details. Often they are moody and easily depressed and see the negative side of things.

Time Tenders always need more time to do things right. Since they tend to be perfectionists, they never have enough time to get everything done. They are usually on time, and they expect others to be on time too. From a time standpoint, they are hard on themselves and hard on others as well.

Their time management strengths include handling details well, being neat and well organized, being detailed planners, seeing potential problems, controlling quality, devising operating procedures, and keeping good records. Their time management weakenesses include being perfectionists, being too negative, getting bogged down in details, being overly analytical, and setting standards that are too high.

Time Tenders feel secure when all their questions are answered and they are well prepared. They do their homework in depth. They resist change because it threatens structure and order. They measure personal worth by precision, accuracy, and thoroughness. They are irritated by surprises and unpredictability. Under pressure, Time Tenders are overly critical, strict, resistant, and perfectionistic, and they often pass the buck to someone else.

Florence Littauer, a friend who has worked with this material for many years, helped us immensely by pointing out the basic aim in life for each temperament.*

---

*Florence Littauer, *Your Personality Tree* (Waco, Texas: Word Books, 1986).

Temperament	*Basic Aim in Life*
Time Taskmasters	Get it done
Time Teasers	Have fun
Time Tarriers	Take it easy
Time Tenders	Do it right

This classification is especially useful in providing insight about how to work well with each temperament.

With this basic understanding about each of the temperaments, we next need to look at how they work with each other. Chapter 4 focuses on how temperament affects teamwork and how each of the temperaments can be more effective. Temperament also affects our orientation to time and time management issues. Chapter 5 explores many of the time management differences among the temperaments.

Some Notes of Caution

We have discussed temperament theory in order to help you understand why different people behave as they do, and to suggest how we can all work together successfully. We believe that the more you understand, the better you'll get along with others and the better you'll work well with them too. Understanding leads to tolerance, which in turn leads to acceptance. However, there are three temptations that we urge you to avoid:

1. *Don't use this information to browbeat or psychoanalyze others.* Although we hope this material will help you to understand yourself and others better, it will not make you an expert on human behavior. Don't get carried away with a little knowledge. Use the information in a positive way, not a negative one.
2. *Don't try to categorize people and force them into a box.* Our aim is to increase understanding, not to pigeonhole people. Although temperament is perhaps the most powerful factor explaining behavior, it is still only one factor. Don't be presumptuous.

3. *Don't use temperament as an excuse for poor behavior.* For example, even though Time Taskmasters tend to shout a lot, that doesn't mean that you'll be excused for yelling. As Dolly Parton observed, "Just because you're a celebrity doesn't give you the right to be a jerk."

As you have seen, each temperament has both strengths and weaknesses. However, we tend to see others in terms of their weaknesses, not their strengths. We need to practice seeing people's strengths and overlooking their weaknesses. For many, this is a difficult assignment.

Unfortunately, weaknesses are also easier to develop. If you're not consciously working to develop the strengths of your temperament, you will automatically drift deeper into the weaknesses. We need to accentuate our own strengths and help others to build on their strengths as well.

To help you learn to appreciate the strengths and understand the weaknesses of your team members, complete an analysis like the one shown in Figure 3-2. Try to estimate the probable temperament of each team member. Think first of what strengths they bring to the team. Then, consider what weaknesses they have as team members. How could you help each one to accentuate his or her strengths? How can you learn to overlook their weaknesses?

Not all temperaments are alike. For example, not all Time Taskmasters behave the same way. Even without considering the influence of other factors on behavior, there would still be differences. It depends on the intensity of the temperament. An 85-percent Time Taskmaster is not the same as a 55-percent Time Taskmaster, although they are both Time Taskmasters.

Environment influences the way you learn to express your temperament. The way you were raised had an impact on your behavioral style. Environment continually modifies temperament tendencies. Behavior varies as situations change. However, we're not dealing with cause-and-effect relationships here. Our discussion concerns tendencies to behave. For example, Time Taskmasters tend to be dominating, regardless of the situation, although they may be more so in some situations than in others.

Figure 3-2. Time teamwork analysis sheet.

Time Teamwork Analysis

List each of your team members. Then one at a time, think carefully about what their primary temperament might be. What are the strengths they bring to the team? What are their weaknesses as team members?		
Team Member and Temperament	What strengths do they bring to the team?	What are their weaknesses as team members?

You cannot change your temperament, but you can change your behavior. In fact, to get along best with others, you need to adapt your behavior to the needs of their temperaments. This is called behavioral flexibility. For example, Time Taskmasters tend to be impatient, but they can learn to be patient. The temperament hasn't changed, but the behavior has. Anyone can learn to behave in any way they want to.

We're All Different, and That's Okay

To repeat one last point—perhaps the most important point: Just because our temperaments vary doesn't mean that one is necessarily better than another. There is a tendency for many of us to assume that because others react differently than we do they must be wrong. Forget about right and wrong. Different doesn't mean wrong, it simply means different. We are what we are. Labeling things right and wrong only makes it more difficult for us to accept each other.

Yes, we are all different, and that's the way it's supposed to be. If we were all alike, it wouldn't work. If we were all Time Taskmasters, we would all try to lead, but there wouldn't be anyone following. If we were all Time Teasers, we would have lots of fun, but we wouldn't get much work done. If we were all Time Tarriers, we might have lots of harmony, but very little enthusiasm and no goals. If we were all Time Tenders, we would be very organized but not very cheerful. All the different parts, working together, add value to each other.

As you continue through this book, please keep in mind both your temperament and the temperaments of your team members. As you read our recommendations, ask how they could be best adapted to you and your teammates. Some of our suggestions will undoubtedly appeal to you more than others. A good strategy for managing time requires building on your time management strengths and shoring up your weak areas. In the end, though, what you do will still be a reflection of who you are.

Anybody can use any team time management tool or technique. However, each person's temperament will affect how he or she uses those tools and techniques. Different temperaments will be more or less drawn to various tools and techniques. As members of a team working together, you can encourage each other as you use the strengths of each person. Everyone can be enhanced as the work is divided appropriately. Using the temperament model as a team tool can lead everyone to happier, more fulfilling work days. It can also help yield greater productivity for the entire team.

4

Temperament and

Teamwork

During the 1960s and early 1970s, searching for personal identity was a popular pastime. Many people asked, "Who am I?" and eventually concluded that "I've got to be me." Sammy Davis, Jr., even had a hit song titled "I've Gotta Be Me!" If you think a moment, you'll remember that Sammy was usually a solo act—and always was when he sang this song.

Teamwork is tricky. We need the individual team members to bring some of that "I've Gotta Be Me!" thinking to the group so we can use the best of their skills to solve problems and meet team goals. BUT. Yes, BUT! But we don't need individuals to think of themselves as the center or most important element of the team. We don't need them to bring a you-against-me philosophy to the team. In fact, we need just the opposite. We need the skills without the personality clashes; essentially, we need the good without the bad.

The good news is that we can get the good without the bad; at least we can get most of the good while minimizing most of the bad. The secret to this everybody-wins situation is the knowledge and understanding of individual temperaments. The problems do not arise because of personality clashes within the group but because of ignorance of those differences and of the dynamics among personalities. Once we unravel the mysteries of relationships, teamwork becomes a true possibility—and we're under way to successfully accomplishing our goals.

Chapter 3 presented an overview of our time temperament categories. If you took the quiz, you identified yourself as a Time Taskmaster, a Time Teaser, a Time Tarrier, or a Time Tender. In this chapter, we focus on how these temperaments interact when working with others in a team situation. We unmask each member of the team. We demystify them. We make them human to the other team members and therefore acceptable. This involves no miracles; all it takes is understanding.

To do this, we must ask some questions. What are the strengths of individual temperaments? What are the weaknesses? How are they motivated? How do you talk to them? What ticks them off? How do you make peace? What sort of situation do they prefer to work in? What can you do to bring out the best in them?

With the wealth of skills brought by individual members, a team can do just about anything. So much can be accomplished! Let's begin by taking a closer look at both the positive and negative effects each temperament may have on the team.

Potential Contribution of Each Temperament

• *Time Taskmasters.* When it comes to leadership, Time Taskmasters love it! Since they also have the ability to stay goal-oriented, Time Taskmasters can lead the team straight to the goal. They can stay so focused that they don't let the inevitable problems get in their way. Their ability to take on risks with little fear can also serve as a safety net for those who are more timid.

However, Time Taskmasters can be harmful to the team by being bossy and quick to anger. Many people may find them insensitive, rude, and tactless. They can also be workaholics with a penchant for rash decisions.

Juggling many balls at the same time is a piece of cake for most Time Taskmasters. They think it's fun. It's a good thing, too, for many of the team's challenges demand staying focused when the world seems to be falling apart. What's more, Time Taskmasters can usually do this with a positive attitude! We need these people desperately; and fortunately, most teams have them.

• *Time Teasers.* Enthusiasm is important, and Time Teasers usually have an abundance of it. In addition, they can also argue persuasively on any given point. They can create a fertile atmosphere in the group that allows other activities to grow. Their ability to verbalize both their own ideas and the ideas of others makes them excellent spokespeople for the team. Time Teasers can put others at ease with their openness. They love people and enjoy helping others achieve results.

However, if you let them, Time Teasers can waste much of their time—and the time of other team members—by their endless talking. This need to be constantly in conversation can easily distract them and make them scatterbrained and inattentive to details. Their lack of discipline frequently causes them to let the team down because they may not follow through on assigned work.

• *Time Tarriers.* These are the ultimate team players. Time Tarriers were born to be supportive, dependable, and faithful to a group or a team. They provide the stability, the cement, that holds the rest of the team together. They are more even-tempered and seldom explode either in anger or in excitement. Time Tarriers are generally very practical individuals who help keep the team on an even keel. Fortunately, they also love to develop specialized skills, and this adds to their value.

On the other hand, Time Tarriers can be worrisome and fearful, which in turn causes them to be stubborn and indecisive. They are usually not self-starters and tend to procrastinate. Frequently, the goal holds no attraction for them, and this makes them indifferent to plans and resistant to change.

• *Time Tenders.* Where would we be without someone to pay attention to the details? This is one of the most important contributions of Time Tenders, who naturally like details. They ask the important questions that prevent so many slipups. They think logically, in a systematic fashion, and work step by step toward the goal. They are not quick to issue a stamp of approval on just anything, but when they do give an approving nod, you know you have a winner. You can also count on Time Tenders to keep track of your progress as the team works toward its goals. They know where the team is going, how it's doing along the way, and just how well it succeeded when the project is finished.

But if anyone on the team is apt to say, "It can't be done," it will probably be the Time Tenders. They tend to see the negatives. They can analyze things to death and get buried in too many details. They are generally hard to please; most are perfectionists. On many occasions they seem too introspective, moody, or even totally depressed.

These are some of the potential contributions each of the time temperament personalities brings to the team effort. Each one has valuable skills to offer, without which the work of the team would be hampered. It is our duty as team members to help each temperament do a particular job to the best of his or her abilities; this encouragement will be reciprocated by other team members. Positive relationships lead to positive results.

Four Ways of Relating to the World

Relationships are a two-way street. One way is how you relate to others; the other way is how others relate to you. When three, six, or ten different people are involved, this two-way street becomes a crowded freeway. The more people there are, the more complicated the relationships become. Understanding the basis for good one-on-one relationships is the most important part of making it all work. Let's begin by looking at how the different temperaments relate to the world.

Time Taskmasters: Taking on the World

Time Taskmasters have one basic aim: Get It Done! If they have to be domineering and dictatorial in order to "get it done," they'll probably enjoy the task even more. Their priority is results, and they pursue them with a vengeance. They are undeniably decisive.

Time Taskmasters frequently have a difficult time working with others. They are generally not "sensitive," and often believe sensitivity should have died with the flower children of the 1960s. They may not be clear on the meaning of the word *empathetic*, but they're not concerned enough about it to find out.

Yes, Taskmasters can be blunt and overbearing, but from their viewpoint, they only "tell it like it is," and others just don't want to hear the truth. When you get two Taskmasters together on the same team, you either get a tremendous amount of work or a tremendous explosion. Taskmasters should understand each other; but unless there is mutual respect they will probably become vigorous antagonists. Conflict, hot and heavy, is a likely possibility. If the two don't feel threatened by each other, however, they can be a great team, mutually respecting each other in an aggressive, competitive manner.

When Taskmasters are asked to work with a Time Teaser, they may moan, "Why me?" The Taskmaster often sees the Teaser as a superficial self-promoter. "Anyone that happy all the time must be slacking off on the job!" They're put off by the Teaser's lack of commitment to the task and soon tire of his "constant glibness." Taskmasters will have more success with Teasers when they learn to be more complimentary and to give frequent recognition for their accomplishments. This can be done without being manipulative—and, with practice, might even become enjoyable.

The complacency of Time Tarriers also gets to the Taskmasters. "Why is he always so indifferent to what happens?" is a likely question. The attacking style of many Taskmasters can repel a Tarrier, resulting in resentment and distrust. Time Tarriers just move more slowly; their bodies respond to the beat of a totally different drummer.

To work more effectively with Tarriers, Taskmasters should try being a little more amiable and easygoing. They should stop pushing all the time. They ought to back off somewhat and learn to appreciate the Tarrier's positive traits. Ironically, once they do this, the Tarriers will probably produce more than ever before.

Time Tenders can *really* frustrate the Taskmasters. Tenders can be nit-picking when Taskmasters want progress, defensive when they want answers, and cautious when they want to barge ahead. Impatient Taskmasters accuse Tenders of "paralysis of analysis." Frustration knows no end!

If Taskmasters want to get somewhere with Time Tenders, they must learn to slow down. They must learn to take all the questions in stride and show that they care about the Tender's work and style. If Taskmasters show that they can be trusted with thoughtful judgments, then, maybe, they will gain the Tender's trust—and be able to pick up the pace, at least a bit.

In short, Time Taskmasters must learn that empathy is not a weakness and that being a "warm" person has nothing to do with body temperature. They also must learn that listening to the opinions of other team members is not a sign of weakness and that compromise is not a matter of losing but of coming to the best possible decisions. They must learn to take the time to explain things properly. Eventually, Time Taskmasters may realize an inescapable truth: that everyone, even Time Taskmasters, must learn to cooperate.

Time Teasers: Savoring the World

"Life is a banquet, and most poor fools are starving to death!" proclaimed Auntie Mame in the hit Broadway musical. Fun, and lots of it, is their rallying cry. Time Teasers focus on influencing and interacting with others. Relationships in the team, as in the rest of the world, is their most important priority. Repeat: It's usually not the task at hand that drives Time Teasers, but the relationship involved. They are basically "people persons" who almost always work well with others, either as leaders or as team members. Teasers are good to have on your side because they can be effective, persuasive motivators and because they generate enthusiasm easily. They may sometimes overestimate their own abilities and the abilities of others, but this can be better than not stretching to reach the hidden skills everyone has.

When two Time Teasers meet each other in a team, they instantly make beautiful music together. Teasers can easily find each other in a crowded department and become fast friends within minutes. When they find themselves on the same team, it's the next best thing to heaven. They will probably become best pals and stick up for each other. Their natural enthusiasm will increase when the other one is around and everything will become more fun.

Teasers may get caught up in trying to impress each other and sometimes compete for recognition, but because the relationship is so important to them, they'll probably decide to "do lunch" and forget about the whole thing. Somehow, combining business with pleasure always makes sense to them, and budget restraints are often overlooked.

Relationships with the Time Taskmaster, however, aren't as much fun. Their charms just don't seem to get anywhere with Taskmasters. Teasers tend to see Taskmasters as demanding, bossy, arrogant, and too serious. They resent being pushed around and may rebel by leaving the team. Time Teasers who want to get somewhere with Taskmasters must learn to be direct, clear, and straightforward. They must focus less on emotions and more on the practical aspects of the objective.

Time Teasers do not have passionate relationships with Time Tarriers. In fact, if at all possible, they'll ignore them. They find Tarriers boring and indifferent. The Tarrier's undemonstrative approach to life is the antithesis of the Teaser's. Tarriers may not be as willing to share their thoughts with Teasers, and Teasers may interpret this as being secretive and possessive. They may also complain that Tarriers are slow.

Patience is a good strategy for learning to get along well with Tarriers. Teasers have to slow down a little. They must also learn to show appreciation for Tarriers if they want to win them over as friends. Once Teasers stop being so pushy, they will value the sincerity and dedication that is the heart and soul of the Tarrier temperament.

Talk about speaking a different language! That's what happens when Time Teasers confront Time Tenders. They simply don't understand each other, and superhuman efforts are called for if there is ever going to be a positive connection. Teasers see Tenders as nit-picky, accusing, and negative. They complain that Tenders always seem to find things wrong or to point out why something won't work the way it's supposed to. They see Tenders as too defensive and too sensitive, only interested in things and not people.

Tenders are draining to Teasers and wear them out. There is only one way Teasers can make any progress with Time Tenders: They must slow down and prepare a factual presentation before confronting Tender teammates. They must be well prepared and remove any threat Tenders may perceive. They must learn to be patient with any and all questions Tenders ask. Teasers must expect doubts and questions, and not resent them. All this goes against their nature, but with increased understanding they will soon see that there are unspoken rewards. They'll like the rewards and be encouraged to continue their painstaking efforts.

Time Tarriers: Strolling Through Life

When Time Tarriers meet another Tarrier, they're happy they've found a new friend. Oh, it's probably not the intense relationship you find when two Time Teasers get together, but it's a comfortable, kind, and patient relationship. Tarriers, seeing each other as just about "right" as people, will be accommodating and supportive of each other. There shouldn't be much conflict between them, but then not much will get done either. "Doin' what comes naturally" is just fine, but if either of them happens to think they should accomplish something, they'll probably need help defining the goals. Once they have a goal, even if it is imposed by some outside authority, they'll work harmoniously together to reach it. They'll be good friends and maybe even get something done, if it's easy enough to get to.

Time Tarriers and Time Tenders tend to work very well together. However, when the Tenders are too uptight, intense, and/or critical, the relationship suffers. In addition, Tarriers may resent what they see as perfectionistic demands from the Tenders.

To improve working relationships, Tarriers should try to help the Tenders concentrate on what's really important and ignore the trivia. Second, the Tarriers can get going faster and allow their natural abilities to show sooner. Once they are engaged, their pace, interest, and attentiveness to details tend to increase, which pleases the Tenders.

When Time Tarriers try to work with Time Taskmasters, it's a much different story. To Tarriers, Taskmasters are nasty, belligerent, arrogant, and dictatorial. Tarriers are shocked by the Taskmaster's rudeness and haste. If at all possible, they will try to avoid them altogether, but in a team situation that will be impossible.

Unfortunately, Tarriers have a tendency to try to get even with Taskmasters and will do all they possibly can to jeopardize the Taskmaster's efforts. Their sabotage may not be obvious, but it can be deadly. They'll score points by getting even instead of screaming back. Taskmasters may never know what happened, but the Tarriers will take silent pleasure in their accomplishment.

If Tarriers want a more honest, positive relationship than that ensured by this get-'em-in-the-end strategy, they'll have to learn to be direct and straightforward. They must learn not to feel intimidated so that they can negotiate their relationships with Taskmasters honestly and directly. With this approach, they can begin to work with Taskmasters. It will get easier with practice, and much easier as the Taskmaster gains respect for the Tarrier's abilities.

On the surface, Time Tarriers may appear to have a good working relationship with Time Teasers, but it's probably not as perfect as it seems. Tarriers often see Teasers as phonies, people who are self-promoting and superficial. They may also see them as inattentive and overconfident. Tarriers take the time to listen and nod when Teasers are talking, but they don't really internalize anything the Teasers are trying to say. It goes "in one ear and out the other," so to speak.

To get more from the relationship, Tarriers should look for the positive qualities of the Teasers. They may not have to look all that hard if they are willing to be open-minded. Once they recognize the Teaser's accomplishments, and particularly if they take the time to say so, they may find a friendship, and a teamship, that is worth preserving.

Time Tenders: Analyzing the World

Time Tenders tend to see each other as smart team members so long as they're perfectionistic about the same things. They praise attention to detail and thoroughness throughout the project. They work well together and have a fairly good time shaking their heads at the inefficiency of other team members. However, they must also be willing to carefully address any questions presented by another Tender.

Tenders have the ability to see small details that can make or break and entire project. The problem is that they may get so engrossed in the details that they never finish the projects assigned them. They may get caught up in being "right" rather than "finished."

When working with Taskmasters, the Time Tender has the same problems as everyone else. Taskmasters appear too belligerent and bossy. Tenders find them arrogant, nervy, and demanding. Tenders, however, may be smart enough and aggressive enough to go over their heads and bring in outside forces to counteract Taskmasters' bold interactions. This, of course, they interpret as a defensive action, something done out of necessity.

Again, the only way to work effectively with demanding Taskmasters is by taking direct, straightforward action. Tenders must learn to stand up to Taskmasters in order to develop a strong working relationship.

Time Tenders find Teasers overly optimistic and tend to throw a wet blanket over them. They see Teasers as loud and empty-headed. They feel that a little practical pessimism would probably be good for Teasers. Besides, it's fun to point out the potential dangers and holes in Teasers' proposals. Tenders often kill Teaser ideas with demands for facts and details.

To work effectively with Teasers, Tenders must be friendlier, listen more, and look for some good. They should stretch themselves and practice tolerance. No one said that Time

Tenders had to become best friends with the Teasers, but, after all, Teasers may be colleagues worth having.

Finally, what can you expect when Time Tenders interact with Time Tarriers? They will probably see Tarriers as too lenient and too easygoing, as people who just doesn't measure up to their high standards. They may admire them for their efforts to reduce the risks involved in decision making, but still see them as lacking precision. For these reasons, Tenders usually ignore any efforts Tarriers make to be friends. They prefer the route of minimal interaction.

If Tenders want to move in a positive direction with Tarriers, it will help if they learn to relax and let things be. If they really want Tarriers to be perfect, they must first try being a perfect friend themselves. This requires that they smile once in a while—at a person instead of a dry joke on TV. That person may just smile back—and it could be fun. By lowering some of their defenses, they may find that they don't really need those defenses after all.

The chart in Figure 4-1 summarizes the likely results of interaction between two people depending on their temperaments. We have shown work tasks (W) and relationships (R).

As individuals on the team become more and more familiar with each other, and more understanding of each other's

Figure 4-1. How temperaments tend to work together.

	Time Taskmaster	Time Teaser	Time Tarrier	Time Tender
Time Taskmaster	(W) G–F (R) G–F	(W) G–F (R) E–G	(W) E (R) F–P	(W) F–P (R) P
Time Teaser	(W) G–F (R) E–G	(W) F–P (R) E	(W) E (R) G–F	(W) E–G (R) P
Time Tarrier	(W) E (R) F–P	(W) E (R) G–F	(W) E–G (R) E	(W) E–G (R) E
Time Tender	(W) F–P (R) P	(W) E–G (R) P	(W) E–G (R) E	(W) E–G (R) E

E = Excellent   G = Good   F = Fair   P = Poor

strengths and weaknesses, they begin to overcome some of the problematic aspects of their temperaments. At this point, they start to accentuate their strengths. This should help everyone move toward more positive relationships. Even those whose temperaments show a poor potential for relating are able to work harmoniously together with positive results. All it takes is the willingness to give a little.

Positive relationships lead to positive results.

We hope that this review of how the various styles tend to react to those around them has given you valuable insights into your own temperament and into the temperaments of your team members. There is really no "right" or "good" style any more than there is a "wrong" or "bad" style. We hope we've made the point that they are all valuable and worthwhile. They all fill a place in the larger picture.

In summation, here's how the four different time temperaments approach the world:

Time Taskmaster	Time Teaser	Time Tarrier	Time Tender
active	enthusiastic	controlled	logical
assertive	gregarious	disciplined	precise
direct	impulsive	friendly	reserved
straightforward	reactive	low-key	sensitive

Memorize these basic styles. You may find them particularly helpful when you're trying to cope with a difficult relationship. It isn't that people are trying to make your life difficult; they're simply trying to do the best they can with their own. Once you truly accept the benefits and limitations of the different temperaments, your personal load will be easier and your personal relationships much more enjoyable.

Dealing With Team Members

Understanding the temperaments is useful when trying to motivate others. Is it possible to get more of what you want? Is this manipulative? Yes, it is possible! And, no, it's not manipulative at all. It is simply using your knowledge in a positive way to reduce friction for everyone concerned. Continuing behavior that is nonproductive and irritating to all is doing no one a favor. If you want to be more successful in dealing with the people on your team (and in other areas of your life as well), consider these ideas for working with the time temperaments.

Getting Through to Time Taskmasters

The quickest way to upset a Time Taskmaster is by being inefficient and ineffective. Of course, just deciding to be efficient and effective is much easier said than done, so you may want to be aware of the Taskmaster's greatest fears as well. If you know a person's greatest fears and you can help alleviate those fears, you are already on the road to a better relationship with that person. The Taskmaster's greatest fear is losing control and being taken advantage of. You can't guarantee that Taskmasters will never have to face these realities, but if you realize that they have these concerns, you can be prepared for possible negative reactions.

When trying to communicate with Taskmasters on your team, deal with specifics instead of generalities. Support all the statements you make with facts. Put them on paper, if you can, but don't turn your position into a big report. Keep it simple and to the point. Don't be problem-oriented. And don't talk too much or try to get too friendly. Remember that relationships are not terribly important to Taskmasters. It is results that count.

Be sure to stress what has to be done without suggesting how it must be done. Focus on results instead of methods. Provide direct answers by being brief and to the point. If you pay attention to these ideas, Taskmasters are more likely to hear you and even to take the action you want. Let them be in charge—and free to do what you wanted them to do anyway.

Making It Enjoyable for Time Teasers

Routine and complexity are the enemy of Time Teasers. They hate doing the same thing over and over again almost as much as they dislike procedures that are too complicated. Team members, therefore, will bring out the best in Teasers if they give them tasks loaded with variety and complete with abbreviated directions. It's not that Teasers can't figure out complicated things; they just don't want to spend the time to do it. It also helps to remember that Teasers fear losing social approval and status. This doesn't mean that they want to be the richest or snobbiest people in the city, but rather that they enjoy the admiration of their friends and want to be respected.

Being a good listener is one of the nicest things you can do for Time Teasers. You may even want to let them interrupt you now and then when they have important questions that just can't wait. And remember, just because you've given them a lot of important facts and information is no guarantee that they've actually heard what you've said or will remember it. The chances are good that they were only half paying attention to you, no matter how important you said your message was. They're not being rude; it's just the way they tend to be.

Be open, friendly, and warm to Time Teasers. Once you get to know them, they'll add an upbeat spirit to the team and pull their weight. The time you spend developing a relationship with them will be returned to you in ways you may not imagine.

Affiliating With Time Tarriers

If you really want to irritate Time Tarriers, just be insensitive or impatient with them. It makes them angrier than almost anything else you can do. Taskmasters and Teasers, particularly, must watch their tendency to be impatient with others. Tarriers readily take such offenses personally, so it's very important that Taskmasters and Teasers take a moment to think before they speak or act.

Tarriers have a great fear of instability. Therefore, when beginning anything new or different, be sensitive to their need for security. Approach any changes gradually, giving Tarriers a chance to get accustomed to the new conditions. You will be much more successful in getting them in your corner if you do.

They also fear direct confrontation; it is extremely bothersome to them. They simply don't like to fight or to deal with an unsettling atmosphere. This doesn't mean they won't fight or can't survive in a negative atmosphere; it simply means they are uncomfortable in confrontational situations. If you want them to perform at their best, you should avoid direct confrontations.

When you are advocating something, don't be too directive or aggressive in your request. Patience will get you much farther. Stress that you are willing to give them all the help they require and that your promise can be relied on. Be sure to listen attentively to anything Tarriers have to say. Be relaxed and low-keyed if you expect to get what you want.

Moving Deliberately to Satisfy Time Tenders

Time Tenders know exactly how things should be done; there is a right way to do everything. One of the biggest irritations, therefore, to the Time Tender is having things in disarray or being engaged in things that may be thought "improper." Tenders are more amenable to your requests and needs when they are sure you're following the proper procedures in whatever you do. They are comfortable with this atmosphere and perform best when they're in it. Their greatest fear is imperfection and embarrassment, so anything you can do to avoid what they see as negative situations, the better they will feel.

When dealing with Tenders, remember to take your time and carefully explain how you came to your conclusions. Don't be vague or casual, particularly in response to any questions they may have. Appeal to their logic and common sense. Be organized, and have the facts in front of you. Make details the backbone of anything you suggest to them—and they will be happy.

These guidelines can simplify nearly all your working relations with team members. If in communicating with them you learn to start from where they are instead of from where you are, you will find your requests falling on fertile soil rather than barren wasteland. You will increase the possibility of a successful interaction many times over, saving time and energy as well.

Figure 4-2 shows our time teamwork action sheet. The purpose of this sheet is to help you assimilate all the ideas we've been discussing in this chapter so that you can easily use it on a daily basis with your team. The more you practice the suggestions we've made, the better the results you'll achieve.

Figure 4-2. Time teamwork action sheet.

Time Teamwork Action Sheet

List each of your team members. Then, think carefully about how to build a better working relationship with each of those people. What could you do? What could they do? Note your ideas on this sheet. Talk to each of your team members and share your thinking with them. Then, be sure to act on your ideas.

Team Member	Ideas I can try to communicate better with team members and to help them be more effective.	Ideas team members can try to communicate better with me, and to help me be more effective.

Remember that everyone has both strengths and weaknesses. Conflicts and misunderstandings are inevitable. With
understanding and acceptance, however, there is hope. We can
achieve greater things together by blending our strengths while
minimizing our weaknesses. We must each strive to accentuate
the strengths of our team members, and complement their
weaknesses with our strengths. When this happens, we'll have
the teams we need and the results we want.

Overcoming Personality Clashes

It's easy to see, even with this brief description of the temperaments, why we clash with each other so often. The Time
Taskmasters can't tolerate the slower, methodical Time Tarriers.
The Time Tarriers bristle at the pushy, impatient behavior of
the Time Taskmasters. The Time Teasers feel like exploding
when Time Tenders demand a precise analysis requiring hours
of tedious work for something that looks unimportant to them.
And the Time Tenders fume in frustration at the superficial
analysis of the Time Teasers, wondering if they will ever see
the point. It's a wonder anything gets done at all considering
that many of us spend so much of our time being upset with
the folks around us! It's all these personality abrasions that we
must overcome if we want to develop successful teams. It takes
not only understanding but positive acceptance.

With these thoughts in mind, let's move on to some
specific suggestions for interacting successfully with the different temperament types.

With Time Taskmasters, be brief and to the point. Confront
them directly and challenge them. Stress results and give them
plenty of authority. Allow initiative, but set firm boundaries.

Remember that in the team setting Time Taskmasters will
focus on the goals and the efforts needed to get things done.
They may ruffle some feathers as they concentrate on the
results more than on the relationships involved. Others must
recognize that, generally speaking, this is the Time Taskmasters' style, and nothing personal is intended. A little forgiveness may be appropriate. However, this is not to excuse their

tendency to be abrasive. Time Taskmasters should be called to task when they become too abrasive or continually browbeat others. Style or not, forgiveness has its limits, and this approach is not the best way to build positive working relationships.

In a team setting, Time Teasers want you to keep it friendly and not to bore them with too many details. They'll respond best if you make it fun. Provide coffee and be upbeat about the project's possibilities. Give them many opportunities to verbalize their ideas.

Like Time Taskmasters, Time Teasers are great at seeing the big picture. They will be extremely helpful with work that involves others, but not so good when there are lots of figures and charts. When passing out assignments, make sure they understand the specifics and know exactly on what date things are due. Be certain you take the time to praise the Time Teasers for anything they do. In all likelihood, they will do even better work the next time.

With Time Tarriers, be patient, pay attention to them, and tie new ideas to old methods. Minimize the risks they perceive. Be consistent and systematic and assure them of your support. Give them as much lead time as possible.

Before you organize your team approach, give the Time Tarriers advanced notice of what is going to happen. Spell out the details, and make it seem nonthreatening. Assure them that their jobs are not in jeopardy, and that the goal of time teamwork is to increase results for everyone. Remind them that they are a valued part of the team.

For Time Tenders, be prepared to provide detailed explanations of why the team approach is necessary. Be specific and show them how all the pieces fit together. Be supportive and reassure them of no surprises. Explain how you plan to help everyone learn to work together smoothly, and how differences will be worked out. They won't want others to drag them down and waste their time. Focus on the positive contributions each person can make to the team. Stress quality and excellence.

Everyone should understand temperament differences, the strengths and weaknesses each person brings to the team. For managers and team leaders, though, this is mandatory.

Peter Drucker put it this way: "Management is about human beings. Its task is to make people capable of joint performance, to make their strengths effective and their weaknesses irrelevant."* Understanding the temperaments makes this a much easier task.

*Peter Drucker, "Management and the World's Work," *Harvard Business Review*, September–October 1988, p. 75.

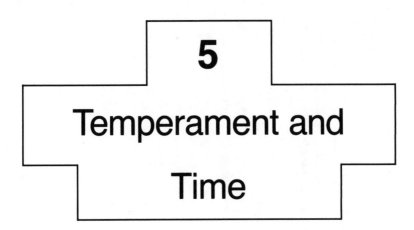

5

Temperament and

Time

Our personalities help determine our attitudes toward time and how we respond to time constraints. For some of us, time is an ally; for others, it's an enemy. For certain personality types, time doesn't seem to matter; for others, it may matter too much. Knowing how different people respond to time management issues can be extremely valuable as we attempt to work with each other.

Each of the four temperaments has a different sense of time—and a different approach to various time management issues. The following chart in Figure 5-1 highlights and compares several of these differences. As you study the chart, make notes that you can share with your team members. Focus first on the characteristics you feel are most like you. Then note down your perceptions of your teammates. Meet together to share your thoughts. In the process, you'll be learning how to work better with each other.

Helping Each Temperament Cope With Time

Some temperaments adapt easily to traditional time management techniques, but others do not. Each temperament, how-

(Text continues on page 63)

Figure 5-1. Approaches of the four temperaments to various time management issues.

Time Management Issues	Time Taskmaster	Time Teaser	Time Tarrier	Time Tender
PURPOSE Setting goals Focusing on goals	Is very goal-oriented, but goals may be sketchy. May not have time to write goals down. Thinks about goals all the time. Tends to have too many irons in the fire and to underestimate how long things really take. Is usually overcommitted.	Will probably develop goals spontaneously, without writing them down. Focuses on current situation; frequently changes goals. Loves to take on new tasks, especially if they are interesting. Tends to follow through poorly and jumps from one task to another. Is often overcommitted and often misses deadlines.	Sets few goals, often because of fear of criticism. Allows goals to create pressure. Usually sets goals when conditions are harmonious, and when others encourage and support methodical goal setting. Works slowly and steadily.	Sets goals for nearly everything and writes out elaborate goal statements. Focuses on procedures and worries about not reaching goals. Tends to get bogged down in the details, frequently missing deadlines.

PRIORITIES	Will set priorities for greater sense of control, but will probably not write them down. Will say no to suggestions that do not match goals.	Talks about setting priorities but avoids doing it, preferring less structure and more spontaneity. Says yes too much; would rather say yes and not follow up than say no and risk the relationship.	Sets priorities because priorities provide order and security, and will probably write them down. Needs time to consider priorities. Avoids saying no; says yes to avoid confrontation and having to defend a contrary decision.	Sets elaborate, detailed priorities—probably too many. Says no because a new task may not fit in with everything else. Needs more information to validate request. Needs proof that it's going to work, or a chance to test it.
PLANS Getting organized Making plans Scheduling	FIRE, AIM, READY Makes sketchy plans; often acts before thinking things through. Tends to be a little disorganized, but will improve to help reach the goal faster. Sees writing things	FIRE, FIRE, FIRE Plans optimistically; tends to act spontaneously. Tends to make unwritten plans and easily forgets them. Appears unorganized, but can focus on several	READY, AIM, FIRE Plans slowly and methodically; needs time to think things through, or tends to get confused. Tends to be fairly well organized. Will get even better organized to re-	READY, READY, READY Makes elaborate, detailed plans for everything. Tends to be highly organized and will get even better organized if the task requires it. Often spends too

(continues)

Figure 5-1. Continued.

	down as a waste of time.	things at one time. Sees writing things down as inhibiting creativity. Avoids the structure that planning requires. Will get better organized if forced to do so, especially if the organizing process can be made fun or easy.	lieve a sense of pressure. Will help if others encourage and support his organizing efforts.	much time planning at the expense of acting.
MONITORING AND MODIFYING	Analyzes quickly, seeing what helps and what doesn't. Evaluates actions in terms of results. Drops an activity quickly if it does not help reach the goal, or if another way promises faster or better results.	Hates details and seldom analyzes; tends to rationalize whatever she is doing as helpful. Will change quickly for something new or exciting, often creating change just for variety's sake. Will probably never	Is likely to avoid analyzing because it's too overwhelming. Needs lots of time to think and evaluate, as well as lots of support. May keep a simple time log if it helps ease the pressure. Changes slowly,	Is most likely to keep a time log, tending to record too much detail, to overanalyze, and to become too introspective. Evaluates actions in terms of proper procedures. Changes slowly unless all questions

	Will keep a sketchy time log, but only if it helps results.	do a time log unless forced to do so.	even when things don't work, and then changes only one thing at a time.	have been answered.
DEALING WITH INTERRUPTIONS OR QUIET TIME	Tends to kill timewasters right away. Interrupts others often, but doesn't want to be interrupted. Interrupts whenever something is needed now. Will try to do other things while talking to you; wants you to keep it short. Creates quiet time easily. Talking helps to clarify his ideas, but he may see talking as a competi-	Generally ignores timewasters. Loves to socialize; would rather talk than work. Interrupts often, but doesn't mind being interrupted by others. Doesn't value quiet time unless pressured by deadlines. Talking helps generate solutions; talks and thinks simultaneously.	Doesn't think much about timewasters. Needs lots of time to think them through. Is overwhelmed by too many problems at once; tends to tackle one thing at a time. Dislikes interruptions because they create pressure and disharmony, but will interrupt someone else when seeking reassurance. Has difficulty creating quiet time.	Since timewasters represent imperfection, tends to criticize them sharply and to become depressed when confronted by them. Interrupts others when seeking permission. Asks lots of questions about details. Takes forever to get to the point. Would rather be left alone. Talking gives permission and affirmation.

(continues)

Figure 5-1. Continued.

	tive situation and try to "win" the conversation.	Talking helps him to think and process information.		
MEETINGS	Likes being in charge, even if not formally running the meeting. Tends to force things through too fast and too often. Is usually on time and fairly well prepared. Tends to dominate the discussion.	Tends to wing it, relying on strong verbal skills. Runs meetings that may appear disorganized or chaotic to others. Is often late and not well prepared. Participates freely, but is easily distracted.	Dislikes being in charge. When running a meeting, usually keeps agenda short and wants lots of feedback from others. Is usually on time, but is slow to participate.	Tends to get bogged down in details when running meetings; has difficulty reaching decisions. Makes presentations that are often too complex and take too long getting to the point. Is almost always on time; tends to prepare well and bring lots of data.
HANDLING PAPER-WORK Cutting clutter Maintaining work space	Attacks paperwork relentlessly and quickly, making lots of marginal notes, lines, and arrows all over the	Tends to avoid paperwork and to do it only when necessary. Tends to ignore the system because it	Approaches paperwork methodically and grinds through it. Follows the system because it lends	Loves detail. Does neat work but tends to get buried in details. Insists on following the system even

paper. Follows the system only if it helps achieve goals, but always reserves the right to ignore the system or to change it for the sake of results. Tends to be cluttered. Displays proofs of accomplishments in office. Office: functional.	means being hemmed in by more structure; prefers to apply own creativity to issues. Displays photos of self with significant people, maybe autographed. Office: cluttered.	security and decreases pressure. May be somewhat messy. Displays pictures of family. Office: homey.	when it is not working. Is usually neat and has everything in its proper place. Office: formal.
PROCRASTINA-TION			
Hates doing boring work or sitting still. Will drop a boring (but important) task for a challenging problem or interruption.	Hates detailed work. Will drop a detailed report for a friendly phone call and justify it because it is important to build relationships.	Hates pressure. Will put off high-pressure jobs to perform low-value, nonpressured tasks.	Hates to make important decisions. Tends to overanalyze all possible aspects of a situation and to research all possible scenarios, often losing opportunities because of delays.

(continues)

Figure 5-1. Continued.

BEING ON TIME	Is usually on time, but reserves the right to be late if something more important comes up. Expects you to be on time and to wait if necessary. Is easy on self, hard on others.	Is often late. Easily forgives others who are tardy because relationships are more important than promptness. Is easy on self, easy on others.	May arrive early or late depending on how tasking the agenda is, but is generally on time. Is accommodating to others who are late. Is hard on self, easy on others.	Is almost always precisely on time. Expects others to be on time and is intolerant of their tardiness. Is hard on self, hard on others.
DELEGATION	Tends to delegate little authority because authority equals control. Tends to supervise closely and to step in to solve problems. Tends to solve own problems, and may unintentionally usurp authority of others.	Tends to be more democratic and to share more authority. Relies on verbal reporting, and tends to forget to follow up. Takes on new jobs eagerly, but tends to fizzle out and miss deadlines.	Will share lots of authority when trust is high or risk is low. Tends to want more feedback, but requires less formal reporting. Needs lots of affirmation, especially when beginning a task.	Tends to prescribe how the job should be done in too much detail. Requires detailed, formal reports and often overcontrols in an effort to avoid mistakes. Seeks lots of details about the job, and will often return with questions to make sure the job is done right.

ever, has its own set of difficulties, and there are ways we've found to help. Look over all our suggestions, but take especially to heart the ideas for the temperament that most nearly reflects yours.

Ten Tips for Time Taskmasters

1. *Take time to write down and clarify your goals and expectations.* You might want to focus on one or two projects at a time by setting priorities. Time Taskmasters often try to do everything, thus losing the ability to do anything well. Learn to listen to and take advice from others.

2. *Think things through before agreeing to take on another project.* Don't be so quick to pull the trigger. Make sure you consider all the details and ramifications. A second thought may be the one that saves the day—and a few other things as well. Are you really the best suited to the task? Consider the abilities of others.

3. *Learn to make realistic time estimates.* Time Taskmasters often fail to realize how long things really take, thus creating multiple problems for themselves and others. Compromise on due dates whenever possible.

4. *Be patient with others.* Don't yell so much. Start earlier and give people more lead time. Be slow to dump multiple projects on people at the same time.

5. *Interrupt others less.* Every little thought that pops into your head doesn't have to be communicated immediately to others. They may be working on something important that you will disturb. Wait.

6. *Try following the system now and then.* It might work. Consider improving it rather than bypassing it or throwing it out. This is crucial for effective team time management.

7. *Pay attention when people talk to you.* Look at them. Start to understand that your way is not the only way. Devote time to seeking the opinions of others and learning from them. Someone else may have a good idea now and then. The strengths of others can fill in for many of your weaknesses.

8. *Compete less and cooperate more.* By learning to work with others, even the sensitive ones, you can accomplish far more than you could ever accomplish alone.

9. *Slow down a little.* Don't be so demanding of yourself and others. Realize that relaxing is a crucial part of good time management. It refreshes you and helps you gain a new perspective.

10. *Take yourself less seriously.* Most things aren't as crucial as you make them out to be. Learn to laugh at yourself. You're probably pretty funny, if you'd only stop long enough to look at yourself.

> Anybody can use any time management tool or technique. However, the person's temperament will affect how he or she uses the tools and techniques.

Ten Tips for Time Teasers

1. *Finish what you start before jumping to something else.* Leaving a string of unfinished projects behind you creates problems for everyone on your team.

2. *Don't use interruptions as an excuse for letting your mind wander.* Train yourself to get right back to the task when the interruption is over.

3. *Focus on developing the on-time habit.* You probably irritate more people than you realize. Besides, there are very few creative excuses left to explain why you are late. It's time to change.

4. *Set aside ten minutes a day for simple planning.* Change "I'm too busy to plan" to "I'm so busy, I *must* plan." Plan at the same time every day.

5. *Once the team has developed a good plan, no matter how sketchy, stick to it.* Don't be tempted to take off in another direction when something interesting comes along. Remember, the team is counting on you to follow the plan.

6. *Try to develop a little more routine in your life.* It is freeing rather than confining because it helps ensure that important tasks get done.

7. *Curb your socializing time.* If you don't, you'll take every opportunity to ignore the work you planned to do in order to talk with your friends. Even though they may never tell you, many people resent the fact that talking to you forces them to work late to make up for lost time.

8. *Simplify the necessary but mundane chores as much as possible.* You may hate doing them, but when they don't get done, you're frustrated. Find others, paid or otherwise, to help you. Invest in appliances, equipment, or technology that will make your work easier.

9. *Clean up your office clutter and throw useless things out.* Make a game of it if that will help. You'll be extremely proud of yourself if you can accomplish this one.

10. *Respect other's rights.* Even though you may enjoy sharing freely the details of your life, many others prefer privacy. They may not even enjoy hearing about you all the time. Learn to be sensitive so you'll avoid becoming offensive.

Ten Tips for Time Tarriers

1. *Learn to set goals.* Start small and work your way up. Good goals add direction and meaning. Focusing on results can turn out to be fun.

2. *Schedule activities to force yourself to start faster.*

3. *Stop procrastinating.* Break large jobs down into smaller pieces and then focus on one piece at a time.

4. *Learn that positive, planned change will make your life better.* Change doesn't have to be frightening. Different can be better.

5. *Be more assertive.* Learn to say no more often. You won't offend people if you do it tactfully. Remember, when you say yes to something you should have said no to, you'll be saying no to something you should have said yes to.

6. *Try to be a self-starter.* Just do something, no matter how small, that you've never done before. It probably won't feel

comfortable, but you'll gain confidence as your team members pick up on your ideas.

7. *Speak up more.* Your opinion is as valuable as anyone else's, maybe even better. Don't keep it to yourself.

8. *Start earlier.* A half hour or even a few minutes can make all the difference in the world.

9. *Don't be fearful of working directly with others.* You'll find a whole new world of accomplishment readily available to you.

10. *Pay attention to deadlines.* Don't be obsessed with them, but don't forget about them either.

Ten Tips for Time Tenders

1. *Remember, although plans are important, it's implementing them that really counts.* If you spend too much time planning, you'll never have enough time to achieve.

2. *Learn that perfectionism has its limits.* Not everything worth doing is worth doing well. Do good work, but stop at adequate. Remember, you're paid to get results, not to be perfect. Perfectionism limits your value to the group.

3. *Try to realize the value of a positive attitude.* By nature, you tend to have a negative perspective.

4. *Be sure your goals are realistic.* Don't set your standards so high that you can't possibly meet them.

5. *Set time limits on your tasks.* Force yourself to do a good job and still stay within the limits.

6. *Remember that most people are not out to get you.* You may just be too sensitive. Learn to sway more with the wind.

7. *Learn to be more tolerant of others.* Constant criticism doesn't make people want to improve. Support the strengths of others. Ignore their weaknesses.

8. *Don't run yourself down constantly.* It's a downer for everyone, and a huge timewaster for you. Ease up on what you expect from yourself.

9. *Realize that some risks are inevitable.* Learn to make deci-

sions on the basis of less information than you would like to have.

10. *Remember that people are more important than procedures.*

Regardless of our temperament, we can all learn to be good time managers and excellent team players. Temperament influences how we approach both issues. Understanding temperament makes it just a little easier to make the necessary adjustments.

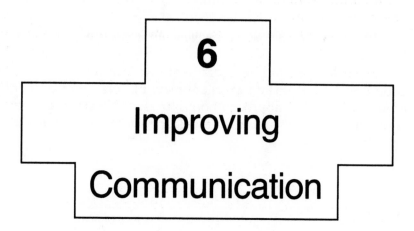

6

Improving

Communication

George Bernard Shaw once said, "The greatest problem of communication is the illusion that it has been accomplished." Those of us who have suffered from misdirection, misconceptions, and misinformation most heartily agree. Our own research over the past twenty years leads us to believe that poor communication is perhaps the biggest timewaster of all.

Just consider some of the ordinary difficulties we face when we try to communicate:

- We may have a limited vocabulary.
- We don't know how to use the vocabulary we do have.
- We are often preoccupied when we speak.
- We speak to people who are often preoccupied when they listen.
- We often fail to think through our thoughts in the first place.
- We seldom say what we actually mean anyway.

When you think of all the things that can go wrong with communication, you have to marvel that any of it is successful!

Clear communication is central to any time management

effort and absolutely mandatory for team time management. It deserves our undivided attention and focus all the more because many of us don't even see it as a problem. Oh, we acknowledge that sometimes we misunderstand people, but we usually assume that it is the other person's fault. Until we recognize communication as the important skill it is, we cannot thoroughly comprehend the impact it has on our time and productivity.

Miscommunicating

Besides Shaw's statement, here are some other common assumptions about communication. Which ones do you share?

- People really understand you when they say they do.
- People understand you unless they say they don't.
- You do a fairly good job of listening to people when they talk to you.
- Your letters, memos, and reports are always clear to anyone who reads them.
- What you do is consistent with what you say.
- You have all the communication skills you need.
- Once you've told someone something, they should "have it."

When you're the sender in a communication, it's easy to get trapped by these assumptions. When you're on the receiving end, however, it's a lot easier to realize that these assumptions are often unrealistic.

Time-consuming conflicts frequently result from these misperceptions. Intentional or not, they arise anyway. Along with our wrong assumptions, we often have differing views as to what is most important and what ought to be done first. We also have differing levels of knowledge and understanding.

In addition to different assumptions and different opinions, most of us readily jump to unsubstantiated conclusions and inferences. Even worse, we tend to accept inferences as facts. Statements of fact can be made only after careful observation. Inferences can be made anytime—before, during, or after observations or, as is usually the case, after no observation at all.

Thirty years ago, Dr. Sanford Berman wrote about a common problem that blocks effective communication.* In his book, he differentiated between making statements of fact and statements of inference, the different characteristics of which can be seen in the table.

Statements of Fact	*Statements of Inference*
1. Can be made only after observation.	1. Can be made anytime.
2. Are limited by observation.	2. Can go beyond observation and indeed do not even require observation.
3. Are limited by number.	3. Are not limited by anything.
4. Lead to agreement.	4. Lead to disagreement.

Wisdom, according to Dr. Berman, begins by knowing the difference between facts and inferences. When we ignore or overlook fact and deal only with inferences, we tend to jump to conclusions. But jumping to conclusions is dangerous! A common reason for communication failure is that people really don't know what they're talking about.

Disagreement is a natural result because most problems do not lend themselves to factual observation and are therefore on the inferential level. Many of us, however, make the mistake of treating inferences as fact and in this way get into trouble. We tend to repeat what we hear, without bothering to check it out. We presume we have knowledge, when all we have is dogmatic opinions.

Learn to recognize the differences between statements of fact and statements of inference. You can do this quickly by asking yourself a simple question: "How do I know this?" Take this question seriously. When you listen to others, ask your-

*Sanford I. Berman, *Why Do We Jump to Conclusions* (San Francisco: International Society for General Semantics, 1962).

self, "How do they know?" Remember that thoughtful people must learn to talk sense when they open their mouths if communication is ever going to be successful.

What Is Communication?

What exactly is communication? Following our own advice, we'd be foolish to assume that everyone knew what we meant just because we used a common word. Webster says that "communication" is a verb, meaning "to give or receive information." We are using the word here in the complete sense of its meaning, not the simple, common understanding of the word. For effective team time management, "communication" means the free flow or exchange of ideas, information, instructions, and reactions that result in common understanding.

Communication involves a free flow or exchange. This means at least a two-way action instead of a one-way action. The more traditional form of communication in organizations has been one-way, directly from the boss down. Unfortunately, it is still done that way in many organizations because, frankly, many bosses like it that way. It's not very productive, but it's quick. It's also nonthreatening to the boss personally. Many managers can go on doing this for a long time before they realize that the problems associated with one-way communication are almost insurmountable. There is a very high probability that their communication will be totally misunderstood. It frequently breeds resentment, and resentment leads to frustration and discouragement. There are few positives from this kind of communication.

Two-way communication is initially harder and more time-consuming. It is sometimes more threatening to the sender—that is, to the boss. But the advantages are clear. Two-way approaches increase the chances that communication takes place because there can be a clarification of the message. The receiver has a chance to provide feedback. When both sender and receiver are involved, you can close the circuit, as pictured in Figure 6-1.

Intentions are what the sender wanted to do or say and

Figure 6-1.   The communication model.

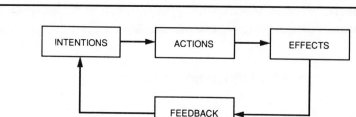

how the sender believes it was done or said. Actions are what was actually said or done. Effects are what the receiver believes was heard or seen, how that belief was interpreted, and how the receiver feels about it. Feedback returned to the sender tells the sender whether or not the target was hit. Put simply, communication consists of what you intended to say, what you actually said, what the receiver heard, what the receiver thinks he heard, and what feedback was returned to the sender.

Communication is a continual flow. This flow needs to be a matter of give-and-take, free from hindrances. The direction of this flow may be up, down, or sideways. Within teams, it takes all these directions.

Webster's definition says there is an exchange of ideas. When ideas are shared, there is opportunity for evaluation and input that can build even better ideas. From each new experience, more ideas can be developed and tried.

Information is exchanged. In any group, there are some people who are more knowledgeable than others about certain topics. Sometimes this is the manager, sometimes it isn't. No one knows all there is to know, so the more facts we can assemble, the better the communication is for everyone.

The dictionary definition says that there is free-flowing instruction. Ideas must be exchanged before any instruction can take place. If the receivers aren't able to understand what is being said, the words are useless. There may be a lot of noise, but no communication is taking place.

Reactions are crucial. Unless people respond to the stimulus of the communication, nothing has occurred. It's best when this reaction happens instantaneously. Free communication flourishes under these conditions.

Successful communication results in a common understanding. This is a mutual understanding of what was sent and what was heard. There must be a sincere desire to communicate effectively, or there will be no success. In team time management, we must *know* that effective communication is taking place. If the exchange of thoughts and ideas is not flowing, we have to find out why.

Responsibility for proper communication is a frightening assignment. It's often easier to put the blame on someone else. Seeking a scapegoat for miscommunication, however, is nonproductive. The ideas must still be communicated effectively.

Rudolf Flesch offers a step-by-step approach to avoiding miscommunication.* Here are his eight points to keep in mind when you are trying to explain something:

1. Remember that nothing is self-explanatory.
2. Translate all technical terms.
3. Go step by step, one thing at a time.
4. Don't say too little.
5. Don't say too much.
6. Illustrate!
7. Answer expected questions.
8. Warn against common mistakes.

Realize that what is self-explanatory to you may not be self-explanatory to everyone else. Technical terms are not everyday language, and unless you know that someone has a very clear understanding of what they mean, take the time to carefully explain. Don't skip even one step in the explanation. In the long run, shortcuts won't save time. Yes, it's hard to know exactly how much to say when giving an explanation, but through two-way communication you will become more and more familiar with the needs of the people you must

*Rudolf Flesch, *On Business Communications: How to Say What You Mean in Plain English* (New York: Harper and Row, 1972).

communicate with. Once you know your receiver, you will be a better judge of how much to explain.

Illustrations are always an excellent way to clarify meaning. The clearer and more familiar the illustration you use, the greater the chance that your communication will be complete. Questions should always be encouraged and answered completely. Your mannerisms should suggest, or your memo state explicitly, that you welcome any questions; otherwise, many people will be afraid to present them and your communication attempt will fail. A warning against common mistakes and misconceptions helps ward off potential trouble and keeps things on track.

Providing Feedback

Feedback tells you whether or not you are communicating well. It is a reverse communication to you that provides information about your effect on the other person. It tells you if your message was received and how it was received. Good feedback enables you to learn good communicating techniques. Knowing how to give good feedback is an equally valuable skill.

To give good feedback, follow these guidelines:

1. *Focus on the behavior, not on the personality, of the communicator.* Talk about what the person actually did or said. You could say that someone talked frequently, but not that she was a loudmouth. Talk only about things you can see or hear. Don't waste time talking about things you can't observe, like what the boss's attitudes might or might not be.

2. *Be descriptive, not evaluative.* Never use language that tends to evaluate or judge the other person. This only inspires defensiveness. Describe your reaction, and let the other person decide whether or not to act on what you have to say. You might say that someone didn't pronounce his words clearly, but don't say that he was a rotten speaker.

3. *Use "I" statements, not "you" statements.* Instead of telling your team leader that he ought to stop yelling so much, tell him how you feel when he shouts at you. "I feel put down

when you yell at me." This is a good way to provide feedback without raising defensiveness.

The only message that counts is the message received.

---

4. *Be specific, not general.* Feedback should be tied directly to a particular time and place. When you tie the feedback to a specific instance, the other person's self-awareness is increased, and learning is faster. Instead of saying you admire a teammate's constant cheerfulness, tell her that her cheerful greeting just now gave you a big lift. It is easier to be specific in your feedback when you give it immediately.

5. *Focus on controllable behavior.* Don't tell people about things they can't change or control. For instance, it does no good to tell a colleague that his nose is crooked. Instead, tell him that the way he smiled and gestured in his presentation was effective and that he should do it more often.

6. *Focus on the present, not on the past.* Don't drag the past into your comments. The more immediate your feedback is, the better it is. Talking about what someone did or did not do in the past is futile. Chances are, they won't even remember.

7. *Inform, but don't give advice.* Feedback is information about the quality of someone's communication effort. The best thing is simply to share your reactions, feelings, and perceptions. When you give advice, you are saying what to do with the information. When you inform, you let the other person decide whether or not he wants to change anything.

8. *Consider the other person as well as yourself.* Some of us tend to dump on someone when we provide feedback. In this case, we may be more insterested in criticizing than in helping the other person to improve. Feedback that serves our own interests more than the interests of the other person can be very destructive and is best not given.

9. *Don't force feedback on people who don't want it.* The main idea of feedback is to improve someone's communication effectiveness. Don't try giving it if the other person doesn't want to

hear it. And don't let someone force unwanted feedback on you either. If you're not sure whether someone wants feedback, ask. It's less embarrassing than blundering on blindly.

10. *Pick your timing carefully.* Don't try to give feedback when emotions are running high. Wait until things have calmed down. And make sure you don't give people more feedback at one time than they can handle.

The Temperament Factor

In Chapters 3, 4, and 5, we discussed the importance of temperament to any team effort. Temperament plays a central part in all communication. Communication is inevitable. You cannot *not* communicate. Communication is both intentional and unintentional. The only message that counts is the message received. Therefore, if you want the meaning of your message heard and internalized, you must consider the temperament of the person on the receiving end.

Along with inborn temperament, each person has a different past experience, which makes each one of us unique. Because of this, every individual brings to any message exchange a unique and individual frame of reference and set of expectations. No two people, therefore, react the same way to the same stimulus. As a result, the message sent can never be identical to the one received.

The role of perception in the process of communication is formidable. Perception is the process of assigning meaning to a message. It's the selection, organization, and interpretation of stimuli. It does no good to get upset because someone misinterprets your meaning. Your task always is to frame your message so that it can be heard accurately and interpreted with the meaning you intended.

The Time Taskmaster personality has, perhaps, the most to gain by understanding the processes involved in communication. A dynamic worker on his own, the Time Taskmaster tends to forge ahead, giving orders to others like a military drill sergeant and naively assuming that real communication has taken place. More often than not, the Time Taskmaster is disappointed by poor results following the attempted communication. Time Taskmasters seldom stop to consider that this is usually their fault. It's their style of interacting that sets them up for so many failures.

For example, Time Taskmasters would see far greater results if they would take time to give credit to Time Teasers and comment favorably on any past accomplishments. An acknowledgment of good work isn't a waste of time but rather an investment in future projects.

Time Tarriers can actually hear what Time Taskmasters are saying, but they will eventually rebel when pushed beyond their limits. Time Taskmasters must learn to understand that Time Tarriers don't appreciate being given immediate demands for work to be finished yesterday. Time Tarriers do best with clear instructions and enough time in which to complete their work. Of course, this isn't always possible, but with the planning techniques we advocate in Chapter 7, you should be able to plan ahead more often, instead of wrestling with so many last-minute rush jobs.

Time Tenders are wonderful assets on any team because they can be counted on to do thorough work. Other team members must be aware, however, that the Time Tender's emphasis on details can be time-consuming and demanding. Team members can frequently help to diminish this problem by paying more attention themselves to details and sharing these details with the team. This can speed up the work considerably and add strength to the project at the same time.

Once we get beyond judging everyone by the standards of our own temperament, we are much easier to live and work with. The effort required to understand each person we communicate with pays huge dividends. Couching our communication in ways that blend with the natural tendencies of our teammates makes successful communication easier. As a result, everyone accomplishes much more, with less effort.

Listening as Part of Communicating

Listening is probably the most important tool for effective communication. It is also the most neglected. People are generally more concerned with what they have to say than with listening to what others say. Learning to listen properly is not something only nice guys do to be polite. Learning to listen well is one of the most powerful ways we know of to get ahead personally as well as to ensure that your work team accomplishes all it possibly can.

Fortunately, learning to be a better listener isn't all that hard. If you practice a few simple steps in your everyday communications, you will find that your listening skills improve quickly.

First of all, learn to focus. Many people believe, incorrectly, that they can concentrate on doing two or three things simultaneously. This probably stems from their experience of doing homework while watching television and talking to their friends on the phone at the same time. They never stopped to realize, a day or two later, that they did poorly on the test they were studying for, didn't really catch the plot of the TV program, and misunderstood something important their friend was trying to say on the phone! Any information is internalized faster and better when your total attention is focused on one issue.

People who continue to think about something else while someone is talking to them, simply nodding "uh-huh" now and then, are creating mountains of trouble. They're pretending to listen, but aren't really doing so at all. One of the most important things they're communicating is that what the speaker is saying is not important. Even worse, they're conveying the message that the speaker isn't important. Of course, no one likes to be interrupted all the time when they're trying to get work done. We'll deal with that issue in another chapter. However, your responsibility is actually to pay attention, not just pretend to do so. You have a choice: Either take the time at this point or suffer the consequences of miscommunication down the road.

If it's worth listening to, give the speaker your undivided attention. Focus on taking everything that is said into your consciousness, and filter out everything else. This is a huge first step toward ensuring successful communication.

Second, your must learn to interpret what you hear. Any

communication is more than just the words spoken. As mentioned earlier, the better we know people, the greater the chance that we'll understand what they're trying to say. Watch for nonverbal signals. Do they agree or disagree with the words? Ask questions and restate your understanding of what has been said. Again, two-way communication is an insurance policy for understanding.

The more you practice your listening skills, the better listener you'll become. Most of us have mastered not listening better than we've mastered the art of listening. Hundreds of books have been written on developing listening skills, and most of them have been largely ignored. To be an effective listener, do three things:

1. Realize that listening is a problem.
2. Give your undivided attention to those trying to communicate with you.
3. Become an active listener by asking questions and restating your understanding of the intended communication.

Do these three, and you'll see a great improvement in your understanding of what's happening around you. This improvement will have a tremendous spillover effect in many areas of interpersonal relationships. You'll also find far less to complain about as more things turn out well and you encounter fewer unforeseen problems.

Developing Dialogue

The difficulties you encounter when trying to communicate with someone are almost enough to make you want to hibernate. It may all sound like too much work. But you simply can't take this approach, for in the long run it's self-defeating. Working with people, in a team mode, is the way to greater accomplishment and greater harmony. The only way to get better is to practice the skills you need.

Try to establish an ongoing dialogue with everyone around

you. You must regularly discuss objectives, intended results, perceived priorities, and appropriate methods. These discussions should not be one-way communications; they must involve a great deal of give-and-take. Dialogue means exchanging ideas without trying to change the other person's mind or prove his or her position wrong. It's an open, honest airing of each position.

There should be a dialogue about how to use time best and about time problems. Find ways to talk about time waste without blaming others. Realize that it's pointless to complain to outsiders about how time is wasted by people in your organization. Talk directly to the people who are both part of the problem and part of the solution. Most of us prefer to talk about issues before we act on them. No talk means no action. However, talking only with those who can't help leads only to constant complaining. Ongoing dialogue must be directed to the people involved.

Dialogue also enhances motivation. You can't motivate another person to use his or her time effectively, work well with a team, or even try to improve communication techniques. In fact, you can't motivate another person at all because motivation is an internal process. The best you can do is to create an environment conducive to individual motivation. If you create the right kind of environment, people will indeed be motivated in the right direction. Regular dialogue is an important part of creating a positive, motivating work environment.

One effective way to get a dialogue started is to ask for help. For example, you might ask others what they've noticed about your time habits, and how you might manage your own time better. Others will always see things about you that you can't see. If you're receptive to their comments, they'll tell you how to improve. This sets up a reciprocity in the relationship that demands that your teammates also consider how to improve themselves.

The atmosphere of your organization is important in improving team time management. Each member must be able to talk honestly with every other member. In a positive, open atmosphere, this is not difficult; in a negative, hostile atmosphere, it may be impossible. Failure to develop an open dialogue will result in poor communication habits, time wasted in activity traps, scapegoating, organizational politicking, and people trying to outmaneuver one another.

Good communication is necessary for team time management. It's the tool that enables the team to work more efficiently. Someone once described communication as the grease that keeps organizational gears running smoothly. Without careful attention to effective communication skills, you'll waste endless hours correcting wrong ideas, redirecting misguided efforts, and soothing hurt feelings. Real progress and top performance demand clear, open communication, which focuses on two-way interactions, empathy, listening, and feedback. Emphasizing effective communication skills will open doors and perspectives beyond the dreams of the old one-way communicators.

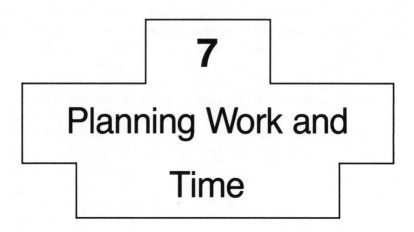

7

Planning Work and

Time

Teams that take time to plan consistently get better results than those that don't. You have a choice: Either take the time to plan, or take the time to fight Murphy. Pay now, or pay later.

Murphy's Three Laws are universally applicable, especially to teams:

Law 1:   Nothing is as easy as it appears
Law 2:   Everything takes longer than you think it will.
Law 3:   Anything that can go wrong will go wrong.

Those who spend more time planning will bump into Murphy less often than those who don't. And teams that invest the time in planning together will reap even greater benefits.

Another good reason for better planning is to avoid activity traps. We sometimes get so caught up in what we're doing that we lose sight of what we're trying to accomplish. That's what George Odiorne calls an activity trap.* They soak up lots of time and energy but give back little in the way of results.

Few of us spend as much effort in planning our time as we

*George Odiorne, *Management and the Activity Trap* (New York: Harper & Row, 1974).

should, even though we say planning is crucial to our success. Bad as this may be for individuals, it is even worse for teams. Working in teams increases the need for planning. What most of us lack is a technique for team planning that is simple and effective.

There are several planning issues facing teams. One is how to plan projects. Another is how to plan time. A third concern is how to coordinate planning and balance everyone's priorities. We'll address each of these concerns in this chapter.

The Basics of Planning Projects

Projects are a common way of life for teams. Your group is handed a job and given a deadline. How you do the job is often left to the group. Good team time management begins when the project arrives.

Be sure everyone on the team understands both the purpose of the project and its importance. The more a project relates to larger organizational goals, the more important it becomes. Questions about the intended results of the project should be clarified before work begins. If you don't know where you're going, how can you decide on the best way to get there?

It's important to involve the entire team, not just the project managers in the planning process. Participation provides several valuable benefits:

- Team members are more committed to projects they help plan themselves.
- They gain a greater sense of accomplishment from executing their own plan than from following someone else's.
- They are more likely to seek improved methods and procedures.
- There are fewer communication problems when everyone is involved.
- There is less competition and gamesmanship.
- There is more flexibility and it's easier to make modifications.

- Potential problems are spotted earlier and often avoided.
- The entire process from planning to completion is often shortened.

Major, complex projects involving hundreds of people are beyond the scope of this book. Rather, we are concerned with the more commonplace projects that all of us get involved in every day. For the professional project manager, there are excellent books detailing how to approach the job.* But for ordinary people, there is precious little written. Most of us just barge ahead, following precedents or common sense.

A project plan is not necessarily a complex document. However, there are several basic questions that even the simplest plan should deal with:

- What is the purpose of the project?
- What are its intended results?
- What is the deadline for completion?
- What are the key activities and milestones?
- What relationships exist among key pieces?
- Who will be responsible for doing each piece?
- How do the team members' temperaments match the project needs?
- By when must each piece be done?
- When must each piece be started?
- What facilities or equipment are required?

Planning is thinking about the future in a systematic manner. It determines what has to be done, establishes the sequence of events, and provides estimates of the time needed.

It helps to prepare a summary project planner, like the one shown in Figure 7-1. You can purchase forms or create your own. Planning is thinking about the future in a systematic

*One of the best is Paul C. Dinsmore, *Human Factors in Project Management* (rev. ed.; New York: AMACOM, 1990).

Figure 7-1. Sample project planner sheets.

Project Planner - Key Activities

Key Project Activities	Time Needed	Start Date	Completion Date	Person Responsible	Resources Needed

Project Planner

Project Name		Date Created	Due Date

Project Team Members

Project Objectives - Intedned Results

Background Information - Mind Map - Diagrams - Notes

manner. It determines what has to be done, establishes the sequence of events, and provides estimates of the time needed. The project planning forms you see must include all this basic information. You may also want to provide space to include simple PERT/CPM charts or mind maps showing the project structure.

There are many excellent computer programs available that enable you to plan projects, especially complex projects. It is not our intent to review those here, although many teams will undoubtedly want to use them. They can certainly make it easier to plot out all the details and to track performance. Our approach, however, is more generic. Whether you use computer software or not, you still have to plan. And even though your formal project planning is on the computer, your personal planning may not be.

There is also much planning that does not require a computer. If you get deeply into the specifics of complex project planning approaches using networking techniques like PERT, CPM, milestone charts, or Gantt charts complete with S-curves, you'll discover that our advice is compatible. If you never learn what these terms mean, you'll still gain major benefits by what we have to say here. In fact, many people using detailed computer programs see our concepts as an excellent interface between the formal project planning processes and their personal planning or team planning.

A Simplified Planning Approach

People often get bogged down in planning projects because they try to think of every step logically, in the proper sequence. Unfortunately, most minds just don't work that way. Rather, our minds skip randomly over the entire territory, alighting here, then flying there, with no apparent organization. And throughout, we worry that we've forgotten a key step or activity.

The result is that we write and rewrite our key activities list many times over as we uncover different steps we had forgotten previously. This is both frustrating and time-consuming. But there's an approach that can simplify the process, ensure that all key steps are covered, and prevent the need for multiple rewrites.

Start by listing activities as you think of them. It doesn't make any difference where you start or in what order you progress. Just list things as they come to mind. Keep going until you've written down everything you can think of. Write each activity on a separate sheet of paper. We prefer using 4 × 6 index cards or the ScanCard® System developed by Marvin Williams of The Executive Gallery, Columbus, Ohio.

Next, go back through each activity step you've identified. Start with the first activity. Ask what must come right before that step and then what must come right after that step. As you go through your list, use these questions to sort out the sequence of all your steps. Asking these two questions for each activity will uncover any steps you initially forgot about.

When you've arranged everything in sequence, go back and assign times to each step. Start at the end of the project with the due date. At each step ask how long it will take to do that step. Ask when it will have to begin in order to be completed by the due date required.

Next, look at each activity and ask who is best qualified to do it. Who would like to do it? Who can do it? What training might be required?

Finally, ask about where it should be done and what materials or equipment are required.

The advantage of using separate cards for each activity is that you can sort the cards in all kinds of ways without rewriting anything. You can also note all kinds of information about each activity on the card. As you think through the sequencing, you may find alternative ways to simplify the process. You may see how to eliminate some steps or how to combine several steps into one.

This approach is easy and it works. The beauty of this approach is that you don't have to know where to start—any point will do. No matter where you start, you keep asking what comes next and what had to happen before. The process itself makes sure that you come out right at the end. You also don't need a computer to make it work, although computers can certainly be useful on large, complex projects. When you finish, you have everything you need to complete the project planner described earlier.

Keeping Projects on Track

Our primary business is conducting in-house seminars for companies. We look upon each seminar as a separate project. Several years ago, when we were conducting twenty to thirty seminars every month, we began experiencing a variety of problems. People were missing deadlines, and all kinds of details were being overlooked. Materials were shipped to the wrong company or sometimes didn't show up at all. Some of these mistakes were causing us to lose clients. We needed to get our team together, and we needed to do it fast.

Our solution was to combine our project planning form with a tickler file. A tickler file is simply a set of forty-three file folders: one for each day of the month and one for each month of the year. Figure 7-2 shows what a tickler file looks like.

When we contracted for a seminar, we would work out all the key activities that had to be done if it was to be a successful event. At that time, there were about twenty-three activities. Each one was identified on the project planning sheet. For each key activity, we assigned one person to be responsible for its completion. At that time, there were eight people on the support team.

Then we worked out a timetable for each activity. We knew the date of the seminar. That was set by the client. The next question was when each of the key activities had to be finished in order to keep things moving at a steady pace. We worked out a formula, based on the seminar date. Each activity start time was expressed in relation to the seminar date. For example, survey questionnaires would have to be mailed nine weeks before the seminar date; materials would need to be shipped two weeks prior to the seminar date.

We next determined how long it would take to do each of the key activities. By knowing how long an activity would take and when it had to be finished, we could calculate when it had

Figure 7-2. A tickler file.

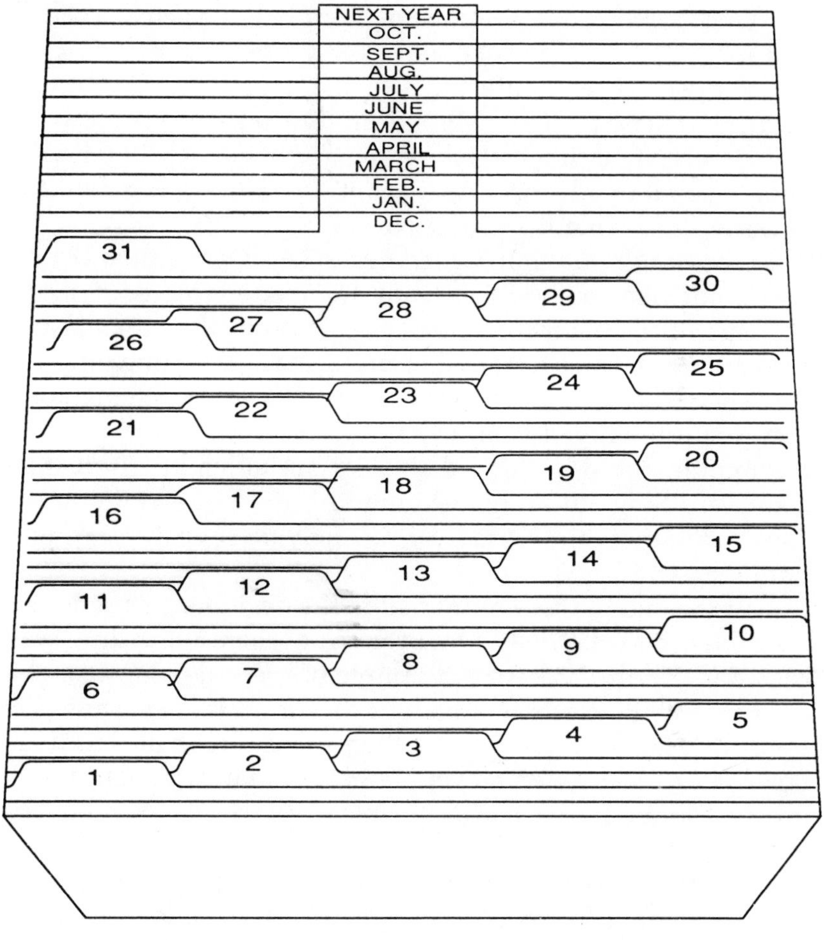

to begin. All this information was written on the project planning sheet.

Next, we made twenty-three photocopies of the project planning sheet, highlighting one key activity on each copy. Then we filed each highlighted activity sheet in the tickler file under the date when the activity must be started. This ensured that no key activity would ever be forgotten.

To use tickler files effectively, there are only two rules to remember: Rule 1: Put things in under the date you next want to see them; Rule 2: Check the files daily. As long as you do that, you will remember every detail at exactly the right time.

Our secretary was responsible for filing the activity sheets and for pulling them every day. As she took them out of the file, she would distribute them to the people responsible for doing that activity. That worked pretty well, but people complained about getting a stack of key activities that they hadn't known about in advance. As a result, these unexpected bottlenecks were slowing the process down.

Our simple solution turned out to be sheer genius. I don't even remember now which team member suggested it. But I do remember how it instantly smoothed out the kinks in our system and solved several other problems at the same time.

The solution revolved around the tickler file. Remember, you remove material from the tickler file daily. At the end of the month, the thirty-one daily files are all empty. You then take everything out of the next month's file and sort it into the days of the month. This is how the daily files revolve throughout the year.

At the end of the month, before the next month's activities were filed into the daily files, we wrote them on a large wall calendar. Figure 7-3 shows a sample of that calendar. It was a 4×8-foot white board we bought at a local lumber yard. We divided it into two halves and then ruled each half into daily boxes. What we had was a very large calendar, with about 6×9 inches allocated for each day, which was plenty of room for our purposes.

We assigned each team member two particular colors. When we wrote the key activities on the wall calendar, we used the color of the person responsible for doing that particular activity. For example, if your color was red, then any activities you had to do were written on the calendar in red marker. By looking at the wall calendar, you could tell which key activities you had to do for the next month. Eventually, we were working a month in advance. At the end of the current month, we wrote up the activities for the month after next. Every team member looking at the calendar could see the key activities they were responsible for this month and next month.

This solved all the problems connected with unexpected

Figure 7-3. Wall calendar project board.

Monthly Calendar

MONTH **Mar** YEAR **1992**

SUNDAY	MONDAY	TUESDAY	WEDNESDAY	THURSDAY	FRIDAY	SATURDAY
1	2	3 LTR AGREE	4	5	6	7
8	9 DESIGN SURVEY	10	11	12	13	14
15	16 PRINT SURVEY	17	18 SEND SURVEY	19	20	21
22	23	24	25	26	27	28
29	30	31				

Monthly Calendar

MONTH **Apr** YEAR **1992**

SUNDAY	MONDAY	TUESDAY	WEDNESDAY	THURSDAY	FRIDAY	SATURDAY
			1 TAB. SURVEY	2	3	4
5	6 CALL CLIENT	7 SEM. FORMAT	8 DESIGN MATZ DESIGN OHT	9	10	11
12	13 PRINT MATZ	14 MAKE OHT	15	16	17 SHIP MATZ	18
19	20 PACK EQUIP.	21	22	23	24	25
26	27	28	29	30		

bulges going through the system. If a bulge occurred, we would back it up far enough to smooth out the work flow and still be able to deliver on time. If necessary, we would bring in additional people to help.

There were several positive advantages from this system that we had not anticipated. For example, by looking at the wall calendar, anyone could see all the key activities assigned to each team member for the month. There was no need to ask whether or not someone could handle other things. You had only to look at the board to see how any particular person's time was allocated. That cut down on many small requests that can chew up team time.

Another advantage was the elimination of progress reports. In the past, we were always asking many different people how things were coming along on one project or another. We hampered their work with all our requests. But because these were all critical projects, we needed to know. Under the wall calendar system, when you finished an activity you simply erased it from the board. If any activity was still showing on the calendar at the end of the day, it indicated a problem. Either it was done, but not erased, or it was not done.

Anyone looking at the board knew what still remained to be done and who was responsible for doing it. Once team members realized that everyone would know instantly if they had dropped their part of a project, no one ever fell behind again. We didn't need written reports or even oral reports. We just had to look at the wall calendar. For less than $15.00, we had a solution that worked well, enabling us to handle many projects simultaneously without dropping a detail.

You can adapt this simple project control system to any number of jobs. It could easily be computerized, although we'd still post it on the wall too. There's something about the visual impact of the large wall calendar that can't be beat.

Planning Your Time Efficiently

The most common time-planning tool is the ordinary to-do list. Almost everyone makes one. Some people write their daily lists on scraps of paper, others use expensive notebooks; some write them up in the evening, most people write them out in the morning. Although to-do lists are better than nothing, they are often not much better. Most are inadequate. Improving on them is not difficult.

The main reason many lists don't work is that people prepare them poorly. Their lists tend to be a random collection of activities that have appeared in their day, often several pages long. Such lists include everything from the key activities of the day to unimportant reminders. Very few lists have any indication of priorities or estimates of how long it will take to accomplish the various tasks set down.

As a result, very few people consistently accomplish all the items on their to-do list by the end of the day. Most people complain that they carry more and more items over to the next day. They feel depressed and guilty as the list grows longer. It becomes a constant reminder of how far behind they are. It is also possible that their lack of accomplishment is creating problems for other team members.

A to-do list prepared in a haphazard manner is actually demotivating, guaranteeing the preparer a future of frustration. The list maker seldom accomplishes all the items on the list. Thus each new list is simply a reminder of the disappointments to be faced by the end of the day. This strengthens people's conviction that writing things down has nothing to do with accomplishing them. It is frustrating to realize at the beginning of the day that all the tasks you hope to accomplish will probably not be finished. Further frustration results when, in fact, a number of the items are not finished by the end of the day. Continuing to write out a to-do list under these conditions is a futile gesture.

The planning system we've taught for many years is significantly stronger than the normal to-do list. It involves asking six questions.

1. What results do you intend to achieve?
2. What must you do to get those results?
3. What are the priorities involved?
4. How much time will each activity require?
5. When will you do each activity?

6. How much flexibility must you allow for the unexpected things you can't control?

Making a daily plan our way only takes a few minutes longer than the time most people already spend on their to-do lists. But the power of our approach is infinitely greater.

To promote good team time management, a weekly plan is even better than a daily plan, although few people ever make one. It provides a longer perspective and allows more room for options. In his autobiography, Lee Iacocca, the feisty chairman who engineered the Chrysler Corporation's salvation, credits his weekly plan with allowing him to accomplish so much.* Ralph Cordiner, when he was president of General Electric, said that if managers would only think several days in advance, they could avoid over half the problems that plague their days.

To prepare a weekly plan like that pictured in Figure 7-4, ask the six basic planning questions for next week. If possible, do this at the end of the preceding week. For instance, you might take time on Friday afternoon or perhaps over the weekend for this activity. Preparing a weekly plan requires only about 30 minutes for most people, but enables them to recover an hour or two daily throughout the following week. An extra hour or more every day for important work will produce remarkable results in almost any job.

Should you do a weekly plan? People doing them definitely think they are worth the effort. They repeatedly tell us about ten benefits.

1. It forces them to think ahead.
2. It helps them to avoid problems.
3. It streamlines the work flow.
4. It provides them and others with more lead time.
5. It allows them to better coordinate their activities with others.
6. It helps them manage staff time better.
7. It prevents overcommitment.
8. It helps them to say no more often.

*Lee Iacocca, *Iacocca: An Autobiography* (New York: Bantam, 1984).

Figure 7-4. Weekly planner.

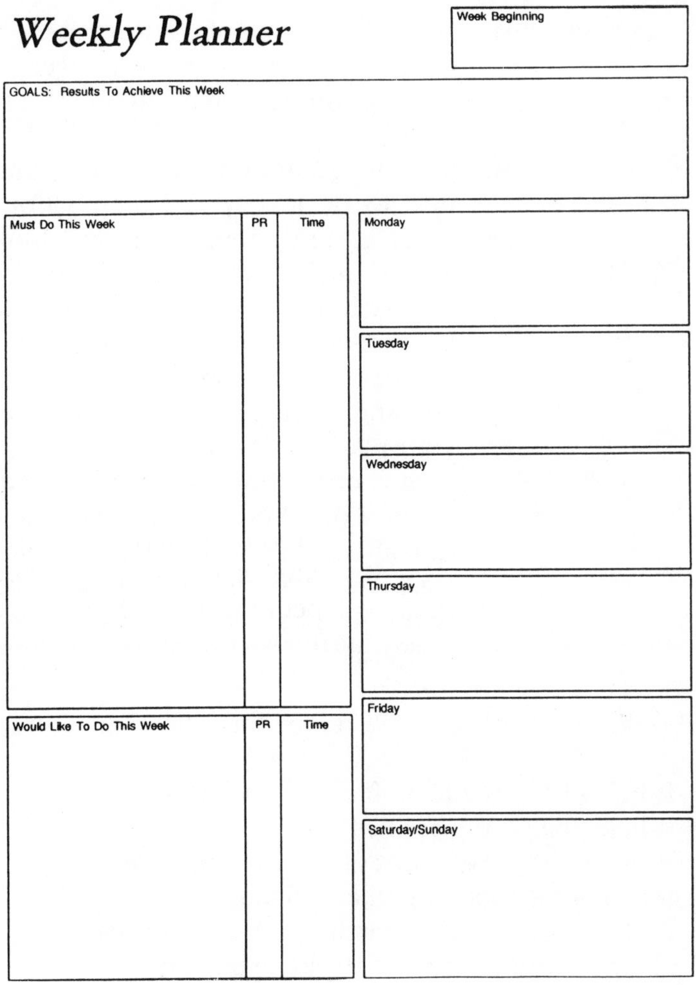

Weekly Planner

Week Beginning

GOALS: Results To Achieve This Week

Must Do This Week	PR	Time		Monday
				Tuesday
				Wednesday
				Thursday
Would Like To Do This Week	PR	Time		Friday
				Saturday/Sunday

9. It makes their work more relaxed.
10. It helps them to get more done.

Now, let's put all this together for team time planning. The whole process—developing individual weekly plans and coordinating them with team members—often takes no more than an hour, and the results seem miraculous. We recommend doing it on Friday afternoons, although you could do it any-time.

Friday, 4:00 P.M.: Ask all team members to prepare their own weekly plans for next week. This will take only about a half hour for most people.

4:30 P.M.: Meet together and share your plans for next week. Just spread them all out on a table, and have everyone look at everyone else's plan. As you're review-ing each other's plan for next week, look for connecting points in the plans. Discuss how to coordinate your priori-ties and activities. If necessary, revise your plans.

5:00 P.M.: This coordination meeting will require about a half hour. So, at 5:00 P.M. you can all go home and have a relaxing weekend. You will already be in better shape for next week than most people ever are.

People trying this exercise report the following benefits:

- It helps keep the team focused and informed.
- It helps balance priorities.
- It increases the amount of information shared.
- It promotes cooperation and teamwork.
- It allows for a better matching of preferences, skills, and abilities with the various tasks to be performed.
- It boosts performance levels.
- It raises morale.

This approach works at any level in the organization. It works between superiors and subordinates. It works with peers. It works with project teams. In fact, it works so well that you really ought to try it with your team.

Coordinating Priorities and Team Activities

Coordinating your priorities with others can be a difficult, frustrating chore. In addition to holding a weekly planning and coordinating meeting, there are several other things you can do to facilitate coordination.

Coordination does not happen automatically. You must force it. When you're planning projects, note the names of all the people who must be notified of changes. Develop routine procedures for notifying them.

Keep the team informed about what's happening and what's going to happen. Do everything you can to focus members on results, not on the amount of effort being expended. Help people to see how their activities relate to the objective and to understand that it's not how much time they spend that counts but what they get done.

Think about whether the things you are asking for will truly overcommit your team, and, by all means, don't expect unrealistic results. Remember Murphy's second law: Things always take longer than you think they will.

If you're facing constantly changing priorities, find out what keeps going wrong and fix it. Constantly changing priorities usually indicate poor planning, poor coordination, or poor follow-up. Realize, too, that leaders who do not have a firm grip on their objectives continually send out confusing signals to the team.

Check regularly with team members to spot future problems and assist one another in handling problems before they become serious. Keep these meetings simple, informal, and small.

Coordinating priorities is easiest when it's done as part of an ongoing planning process. People who don't regularly talk about plans and priorities with each other have great difficulty coordinating things with others. All too often we think that it's someone else's job to coordinate with us. Instead, assume it's your responsibility, and do it promptly.

Planning for Systemic Improvement

Group Productivity

Total quality management (TQM) is one of the current trends in business. Japanese companies pioneered the concept by showing how TQM improves one's competitive position. Organizations wanting to compete must take total quality seriously. Team time management is an important part of TQM.

Coordination does not happen automatically.
You must force it.

Continually think about how to do things better. Keep asking your team members for ideas on how to improve operations and procedures. Hold brainstorming sessions regularly. For example, you might have your team brainstorm this question: "How might we develop more effective team meetings?"

Walt Disney used to tack problems to the office bulletin board each day as a challenge to his staff. As ideas occurred to people, they would scribble their thoughts on a piece of paper and tack it up on the board. When the various solutions had been collected, the staff would evaluate the ideas and pick the best ones. Many companies do something similar by putting the problem on their computer bulletin board. In this way, thousands of people see what the company is trying to solve, and some are likely to have ideas that might help.

The Total System

Another concern of team time management is the performance of the larger system—the whole department, division, or company—of which the team is a part. Common sense tells us that the way to maximize total system performance is to maximize the performance of each of its pieces. In other words, if each person manages his or her time well, then the entire department will function at its best. Sometimes this is true, but often it isn't.

General systems theory introduced the idea of suboptimization. In order to maximize the total system performance, you may have to operate some parts of the system at less than maximum capacity. We often call this compromising. In their book, *The Goal*, authors Eliyahu Goldratt and Jeff Cox applied this kind of thinking with startling results.* They maintain that no system functions faster than the slowest component. Speeding up other components in the system will not improve the total system, and will actually increase costs.

Suppose, for example, that your department makes one part of a product. Your goal is to operate your department with maximum efficiency. You reason that the more parts you turn out per hour, the greater the productivity and the lower the per unit cost of the parts produced. However, let us also suppose that the rest of the assembly line can't keep pace, they can't use the parts as fast as you can produce them. As a result, the extra parts created pile up in inventory.

The problem is that the cost of carrying the excess inventory is greater than the savings generated by running your department at maximum efficiency. Although you have maximized your part, the total system suffers. Unless the entire process can be speeded up, the total company would be much better off if your department were operated at less than maximum efficiency to match the pace of the assembly process. In other words, by making one part inefficient, you make the total more effective.

While this may all be true, trouble quickly looms on the horizon. The goal structure may reward department managers for maximizing their own department efficiencies. Many of us assume that if we maximize each of the parts, we will automatically maximize the total. Sometimes that's true, but often it isn't. And even when we know what's needed, it somehow doesn't seem right to be purposefully inefficient. Ego, pride, preoccupation with self, and even common sense can prevent

*Eliyahu M. Goldratt and Jeff Cox, *The Goal: A Process of Ongoing Improvement* (rev. ed.; New York: North River Press, 1986).

us from accepting some inefficiencies from ourselves in order to benefit the total system.

Thus, working to improve individuals or teams in isolation from the larger whole is not always useful and can sometimes be counterproductive. A better approach is to work on improving the total system. We must examine the system as a whole and study the parts in relation to each other.

A Group Perspective

Planning for effective group performance is not just another difficult, time-consuming chore. Working as a definite part of a group provides the security, perspective, and support you need to achieve the best results. It is mandatory for achieving both group and personal goals.

There is a big difference between the team time management approach and the individual ways of the past. Team time management requires an emphasis on the values and perspectives of the team. For some people, this represents a major shift in habits and natural inclinations. For others, such an outlook is almost automatic. But for everyone involved, the planning of time and work at a group level will prove to be well worth any initial investment it may require.

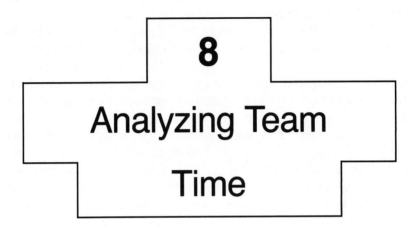

8

Analyzing Team

Time

People often misperceive the nature of their time problems because they fail to analyze how their time is spent. Things are not what they think they are. When we ask people to describe their jobs as they think they are, they draw up a list of the job's components, but when they compare this list with an actual record of what they do, they're usually surprised at the large difference between the two. In *The Sign of the Four*, Sherlock Holmes chides Dr. Watson by saying, "Watson, you see, but you do not observe." A similar admonition could be applied to most people. They're so accustomed to doing the things they do, day in and day out, that they act without either thinking or knowing.

If you're like most people, you *think* you know more about how you spend your time than you actually do. We tend to believe that our memories are "good enough" for a fairly accurate account of the hours and minutes we spend on a given task. However, time after time, people come up short when put to the test. Would you expect a doctor to prescribe a cure without diagnosing the problem? The same thing holds for your team too. You can't prescribe effective time cures without first diagnosing the time problems.

Habitual behavior consumes a great deal of our time, as much as 80 to 90 percent according to some researchers. This behavior is often unconscious. Although we may claim to remember where our time goes, countless studies have demonstrated that we don't do so accurately. Sometimes our estimates are so far off the mark as to be useless. So we can't even gauge our own time expenditures accurately, how can we possibly judge how others spend their time?

There's another problem involved. Because we fail to perceive time use accurately, we frequently think of it as beyond our control. No doubt some of it is beyond our control, but there is still much that we can do with the rest of it. Before we can control time, though, we must understand how it is actually being used. We must also be willing to accept the fact that we cause many time problems for each other.

No problem can be solved until it is well defined. Quite often, by trying to solve the problem we think we have, we end up solving the wrong problem or make the existing problem worse. Good information about time use leads to good problem definition, which in turn leads to good solutions.

Doing a team time/task analysis can be extremely valuable. It helps you to see where total team time is spent. It shows you where there may be duplication of effort. It helps you to figure out how to allocate everyone's time better and how to fine-tune the team's operation. This is especially critical if your organization has recently been through a downsizing, with fewer people left to do the work.

Some companies make a fundamental error as they become leaner. The mistake is believing that fewer people can do everything the larger staff did—and do it in the same way too. These companies expect everyone to do more and to do it faster, while at the same time insisting that everyone follow the same rules and procedures as before. That's crazy.

Why not take the thinning process as a golden opportunity to improve systems? Why not simplify and streamline procedures? Why not change the rules and regulations? Perpetuating the status quo with a smaller staff only leads to longer hours and more frustration. No wonder the results are often so meager.

Team Time/Task Analysis

The team time/task analysis is designed to help any team improve. It gets everyone thinking about how to improve without pointing the blame at anyone. Done well, it can be a positive morale and productivity booster. It has six steps:

1. *Begin your analysis by asking several fundamental questions:*

- What are we trying to achieve?
- What's important and what isn't?
- What are the priorities?
- What can we safely eliminate?
- How well must various functions be done?
- What can we simplify and streamline?
- What can be modified or combined?

Everyone needs to know the answer to these questions. Otherwise, there is sure to be a lot of floundering around in the dark. Answers to these questions help provide the criteria for sorting out the data that come later.

2. *Ask team members to list all the different tasks that form part of their jobs.* Most people will need only 15 to 20 minutes to list everything they can think of. However, this initial list will not include everything. So, for the next week, ask them to keep adding tasks to their lists as they remember them. Figure 8-1 pictures a sample task-activity list.

3. *Combine all the individual task lists generated by Step 2 into one master task list.* This will show the tasks being done by each person. Give all team members a copy of the master task list and ask them to study it carefully. Does the distribution of the work seem reasonable? What duplications show up? Are people doing tasks that are no longer necessary? Try to eliminate anything that doesn't add value.

4. *Ask everyone to record how much time they spend on each of their tasks.* Use the task lists from Step 2 to develop a matrix time log like the one shown in Figure 8-2. To log time, all that's required is to place a check mark by a specific task for every

Figure 8-1. Sample task-activity list.

Task - Activity List

Name		Job		Date	
Project	Task No.		Tasks - Activities		

15-minute time segment, then ask team members to summarize their activities at the end of the week and to give you a summary similar to the one in Figure 8-3.

Keeping time logs requires the team's positive cooperation, which can be obtained fairly easily if the team leader actively participates in the exercise, rewards people for accurately reporting their activities, and never uses log data to criticize or penalize people. The purpose of the logs is to find and fix

Figure 8-2. Matrix time log.

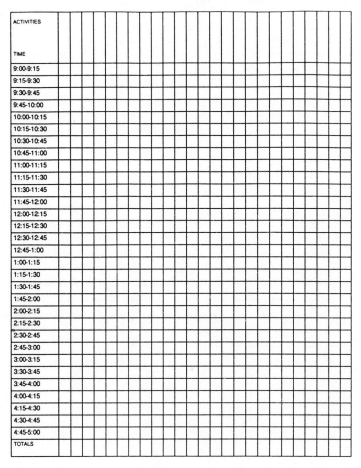

Matrix Time Log

ACTIVITIES TIME																												
9:00-9:15																												
9:15-9:30																												
9:30-9:45																												
9:45-10:00																												
10:00-10:15																												
10:15-10:30																												
10:30-10:45																												
10:45-11:00																												
11:00-11:15																												
11:15-11:30																												
11:30-11:45																												
11:45-12:00																												
12:00-12:15																												
12:15-12:30																												
12:30-12:45																												
12:45-1:00																												
1:00-1:15																												
1:15-1:30																												
1:30-1:45																												
1:45-2:00																												
2:00-2:15																												
2:15-2:30																												
2:30-2:45																												
2:45-3:00																												
3:00-3:15																												
3:30-3:45																												
3:45-4:00																												
4:00-4:15																												
4:15-4:30																												
4:30-4:45																												
4:45-5:00																												
TOTALS																												

problems, not to fix blame. If they are used for any other end, team members are likely to keep inadequate records, alter the logs to make themselves look better, or destroy the usefulness of the exercise in some other way.

5. *At the end of the week, develop a master task-time matrix for the entire team.* In the one shown in Figure 8-4, the rows show the total number of tasks for everyone on the team, while the

Figure 8-3. Weekly task summary.

Weekly Task Summary

Name	Job	Week Ending

Project	Task No.	Tasks - Activities	Hours

columns indicate how much time each person spent on various tasks during the week.

A computer spreadsheet program makes it easy to compile the matrix report. Line totals show the total time spent on any one task, no matter how many team members were involved, and column totals show the total time spent by each team member.

Figure 8-4. Master task-time matrix.

Master Task - Time Matrix (A)

Master Task List	Name	Name	Name	Name	Name

Master Time - Task Matrix (B)

Name	Name	Name	Name	Name	Name	Name

Master Task - Time Matrix (C)

Name	Name	Name	Name	Name	Name	TOTAL TIME

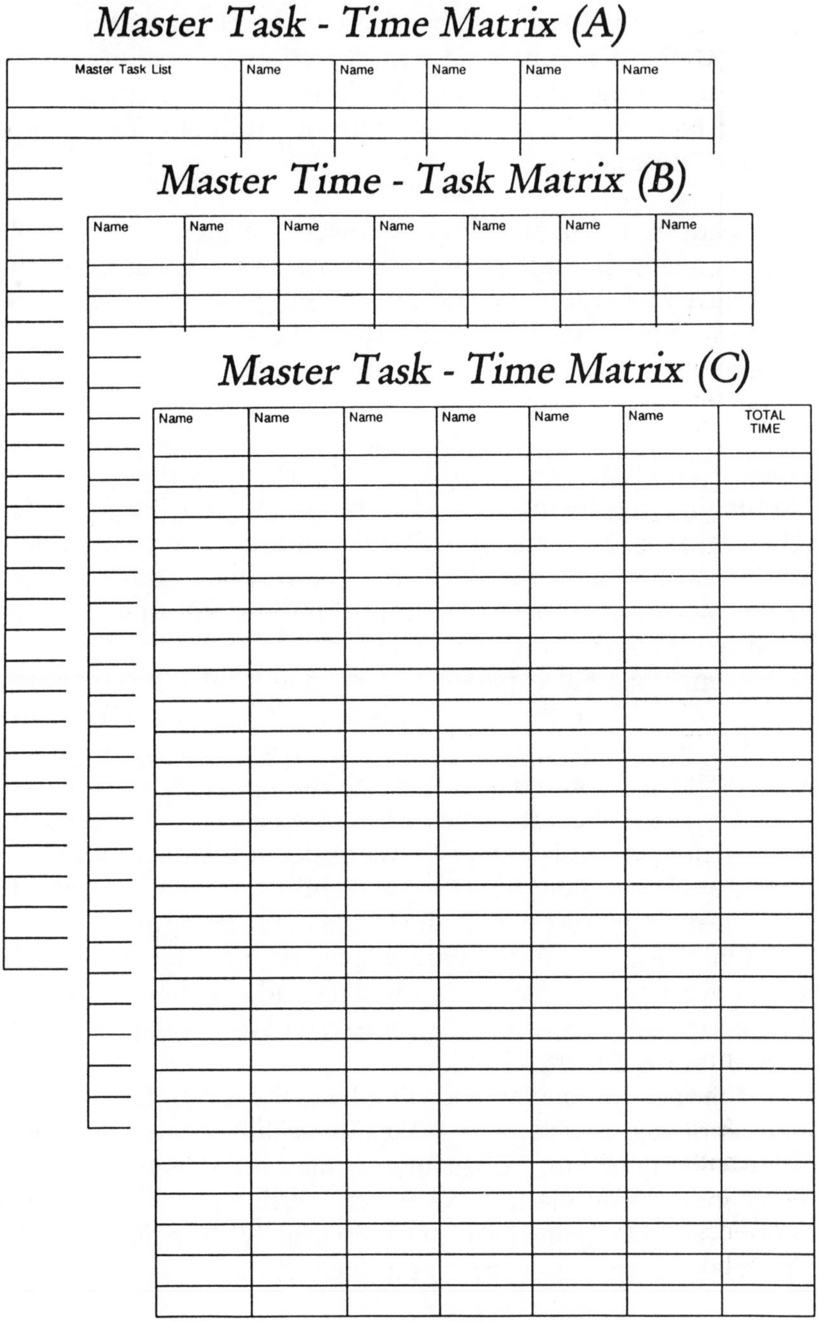

6. *Give all team members a copy of the final report.* Ask them to review it carefully. Then, meet together to discuss any suggestions for improving work flow. Discussion should be centered on what is being done, where it is being done, when it is being done, how it is being done, who is doing it, how long it takes them, and what value it produces. This is the heart of the analysis.

Team time/task analysis is a powerful exercise. Done well, it never fails to point to possible improvements. It's an excellent approach to fine-tuning and streamlining jobs. And because team members have been involved every step of the way, it becomes relatively simple to implement the changes decided on.

The biggest problem is bosses who won't abide by the rules. Too often, they try to ignore them. They don't want to do the time log themselves. They can't stop criticizing people. They seldom say thank-you. But if you are a team leader and can't or won't follow the rules, don't even attempt this exercise. It will not only be a big waste of time but will upset all the participants in the bargain.

From personal experience, we know that it's sometimes difficult to stick to the rules. This is especially true when you see something you don't like. We've developed a system for making it easier on ourselves. Here's our approach.

First, we collect the weekly time logs on Friday afternoon, just as people are leaving. We thank team members for their cooperation. We now have the weekend to compile the data. It also means that we can yell all we like at the computer.

On Monday, we distribute copies of the total report. We thank everyone for recording the data and ask them to review the report for a day or so. On Tuesday or Wednesday, we meet to discuss the report.

The meeting begins with thanking the group for its accurate reporting, which alone makes this exercise possible. Then we ask the question, "Does anyone have any positive suggestions for improvement?" We never criticize anything on the report—neither collectively nor individually. Nor do we allow anyone in the group to criticize anyone else.

If you want to make strong, positive improvements, you need accurate data. When people trust you, they report honestly; when they don't trust you, they won't. When people are comfortable with honest reporting, you can cut right to the heart of issues. Improvements come much easier and faster.

Thomas Edison said,
"There is always a better way to do anything.
It's up to you to find it."

Improving Procedures

Although for most of us there is room for improvement in many of the procedures we use at work, few of us rush to embrace innovation. We simply continue to do things the way we've always done them, no matter how inefficient that way is. Thomas Edison said, "There is always a better way to do anything. It's up to you to find it." We believe this is true for almost anything we do in our offices. The question is simply whether we want to look for ways of improving our procedures.

Improvements are both more fun and easier to implement when we work on them as a team. When everyone participates, understanding, mutual respect, and confidence flourish, while resistance and resentment are minimized.

We believe that when the conditions are right most people like to work in groups. In groups, people learn from each other. Everyone has a chance to participate and affect the nature of the work. Approached this way, the improvements belong to the group. What we own we take care of best.

We believe that most people want to improve. In fact, most of us have been striving for improvement since we were small children. Given the opportunity, we enjoy applying our creativity to finding new and better ways to accomplish the job. Improving is as natural as breathing.

Most of us do not resist changing so much as we resist

being changed. Participation is important in the change process. Most people want to enjoy their work, and they want to do something they can be proud of. What really frustrates people is seeing how things could be done better and still being forced by bureaucratic nonsense to do them in a worse way.

During the 1950s and 1960s, work simplification workshops were popular in this country. Work simplification was a term coined by professor Erwin Schell of M.I.T., defined as "the organized application of common sense to find easier ways of doing work."* These workshops taught simple ways of examining processes and looking for possible improvements. The techniques are just as valid today, although most people have never heard of them.

One of our favorite work simplification tools is the flow process chart. It's easy to use and anyone can handle it. It graphically shows an entire process, or some portion of that process. It's a bird's-eye view of what's happening. By breaking things down into discrete steps, it makes it easier to see possible improvements.

There are several steps in developing a flow process chart, an example of which is shown in Figure 8-5:

1. Select the job or process to be studied.
2. Decide on a place to start and a place to end.
3. Make a brief description of each step in the process.
4. Apply symbols to illustrate the steps.
5. Note any quantities, distances moved, or times involved.
6. Make a flow diagram.

In Figure 8-5 there are five symbols in play. These standard symbols on the flow process chart allow you to indicate what is happening at each step of a process. When the total job has been broken down into its component parts, you will only need one symbol for each detail.

---

*From the author's notes at a work simplification seminar in 1963 at Union Bank in Los Angeles.

Figure 8-5. Flow process chart for filling out and approving Form X.

FLOW PROCESS CHART				NO. 1 PAGE 1 OF 1	

SUMMARY

	PRESENT		PROPOSED		DIFFERENCE	
	NO.	TIME	NO.	TIME	NO.	TIME
○ OPERATIONS	15					
⇨ TRANSPORTATIONS	2					
☐ INSPECTIONS	2					
D DELAYS	5					
▽ STORAGES	1					
DISTANCE TRAVELED	600 FT.		FT.		FT.	

JOB ___Fill Out and Approve Form X___

☐ MAN OR ☑ MATERIAL ___Form X___

CHART BEGINS ___In A's desk drawer___

CHART ENDS ___In A's out drawer___

CHARTED BY ___AHM___ DATE ___

DETAILS OF (Percent Proposed) METHOD	OPERATIONS / TRANSPORT / INSPECTION / DELAY / STORAGE / DISTANCE IN FEET / QUANTITY / TIME / ELIMINATE / COMBINE / STORE / PLACE / PERSON / IMPROVE	NOTES
1 In A's desk drawer	○⇨☐ D ▼	No definite location
2 Removed and placed on desk	○⇨☐D▽	Disorderly desk
3 Filled out	●⇨☐D▽	Original & 4 copies
4 Placed in OUT box	○⇨☐D▽	Long reach
5 Waits	○⇨☐D▽	For messenger pick up
6 Picked up by messenger	○⇨☐D▽	Difficult grasp
7 To B's office	○⇨☐D▽	Delay in rest room
8 Placed in IN box	○⇨☐D▽	
9 Waits	○⇨☐D▽	
10 Picked up by by B	○⇨☐D▽	Difficult grasp
11 Examined	○⇨☐D▽	
12 Signed	●⇨☐D▽	
13 Placed in OUT box	○⇨☐D▽	Long reach
14 Waits	○⇨☐D▽	For pick-up
15 Picked up by messenger	○⇨☐D▽	Difficult grasp
16 Back to A	○⇨☐D▽	
17 Placed in IN box	○⇨☐D▽	Location of box bad
18 Waits	○⇨☐D▽	
19 Picked up by A	○⇨☐D▽	
20 Read	○⇨☐D▽	
21 Paper clips removed	○⇨☐D▽	
22 Carbons and copies separated	○⇨☐D▽	
23 Reassembled	○⇨☐D▽	
24 Placed in OUT box	○⇨☐D▽	Long reach
25 Waits	○⇨☐D▽	For messenger pick up

○   The OPERATION symbol means that something is being done with the object at this step.

●   The "DO" OPERATION symbol is indicated by filling in the center of the OPERATION symbol. When this is done, it indicates that something is created, or added to or subtracted from the object at this step. In other words, the object is changed in some way.

⇨   The TRANSPORTATION symbol indicates that the object is being moved from one location to another.

▢   The INSPECTION symbol shows that something is being checked or verified.

◗   The DELAY symbol indicates waiting. The flow or movement of the object is interrupted or delayed, and nothing is happening.

▽   The STORAGE symbol is used to show that the object has been put where it belongs.

Here are several guidelines for effective charting:

- Don't attempt to cover too much ground.
- Make charts on the scene and try to watch the actual process in operation. Charting from memory leads to mistakes.
- Be consistent on how much detail you show.
- Stick to the subject, and don't confuse things by trying to mix two processes together.

The flow process chart breaks down the process into simple, individual details that make the process stand out clearly. This condensed form makes it easy for anyone to visualize the entire process from beginning to end. Using the chart, it is easier to spot possible improvements. Sometimes the improvements become obvious as soon as one makes the observations necessary to draw up the chart.

As you look over the process, challenge every detail. Study the process carefully for any possible improvements. Ask these critical questions:

WHAT?   What is the purpose of doing this? Why should it be done?

WHERE?   Where is this being done? Why is it being done there? Where is the best place to do it? Why should it be done there?

WHEN?   When is it being done? Why is it being done then? When is the best time to do it? Why should it be done then?

WHO?   Who does it? Why does he do it? Who should do it? Why should she do it?

HOW?   How is it being done? Why is it done this way? Is there a better way to do it?

Question each step separately. Look for backtracking, unnecessary movement, and bottlenecks. Check to see if the right people are doing it. Look for anything that can be eliminated. Ask if any steps can be combined. Consider changing the sequence, the place, or the person. Finally, prepare another flow process chart illustrating the new process. Figures 8-6 and 8-7 picture alternative ways in which the process shown in Figure 8-5 might be improved. Note the significant differences in the summary box.

The process shown in Figure 8-6 is a big improvement over the one described in Figure 8-5. There are fewer steps, the object travels a shorter distance, and the total time for completion was shortened from 25 to 15 minutes. However, the process shown in Figure 8-7 is still better. The original twenty-five steps have been reduced to only six steps, and the total time needed to complete the process has been reduced from 25 minutes to 6 minutes. This illustrates the value of charting a process and looking for possible improvements.

These three flow charts also illustrate another point. When we're trying to improve something, we tend to latch onto the first improvement we can see. However, there is often an even better improvement, if we only keep looking. Our tendency to stop with the first good idea often prevents us from getting to the best idea.

Figure 8-6.   Improved flow process chart for filling out and approving Form X.

| FLOW PROCESS CHART | | | | | | | NO. ___2___ PAGE _1_ OF _1_ |

SUMMARY

	PRESENT		PROPOSED		DIFFERENCE		
	NO.	TIME	NO.	TIME	NO.	TIME	
○ OPERATIONS	15		9		6		
⇨ TRANSPORTATIONS	2		1		1		
☐ INSPECTIONS	2		1		1		
D DELAYS	5		3		2		
▽ STORAGES	1		1		0		
DISTANCE TRAVELED	600 FT.		300 FT.		300 FT.		

JOB ___Fill Out and Approve Form X___

☐ MAN OR ☑ MATERIAL ___Form X___

CHART BEGINS ___In A's desk drawer___

CHART ENDS ___In B's out drawer___

CHARTED BY ___AHM___   DATE _____

POSSIBILITIES

DETAILS OF (Percent Proposed) METHOD	OPERATIONS / TRANSPORT / INSPECTION / DELAY / STORAGE	DISTANCE IN FEET	QUANTITY	TIME	CHANGE: ELIMINATE / COMBINE / STORE / PLACE / PERSON / IMPROVE	NOTES
1 In A's desk drawer	○⇨☐ D ▼					
2 Removed and placed on desk	○⇨☐D▽					
3 Filled out	●⇨☐D▽					Original & 4 copies
4 Placed in OUT box	○⇨☐D▽					Long reach
5 Waits	○⇨☐D▽					For messenger pickup
6 Picked up by messenger	○⇨☐D▽					Difficult grasp
7 To B's office	○⇨☐D▽	300				
8 Placed in IN box	○⇨☐D▽					
9 Waits	○⇨☐D▽					
10 Picked up by by B	○⇨☐D▽					Difficult grasp
11 Examined	○⇨☐D▽					
12 Signed	●⇨☐D▽					
13 Carbons and copies separated	○⇨☐D▽					
14 Placed in OUT box	○⇨☐D▽					Long reach
15 Waits	○⇨☐D▽					
16	○⇨☐D▽					
17	○⇨☐D▽					
18	○⇨☐D▽					
19	○⇨☐D▽					
20	○⇨☐D▽					
21	○⇨☐D▽					
22	○⇨☐D▽					
23	○⇨☐D▽					
24	○⇨☐D▽					
25	○⇨☐D▽					

Team Time/Talent Assessment

People are more likely to dedicate themselves to goals that they set for themselves. They will work on projects assigned to them, but not always with the same commitment as when they participate in the decision-making process concerning the project. This concept is crucial to effective team time management. People achieve more in less time, and are happier with their work, when they can match their individual talents and preferences to the needs of the team.

Rigid job descriptions often become a barrier to the flexibility required by a well-functioning team. The team time/talent assessment is a useful tool for reorganizing your team so that it can achieve maximum results. It may be just what you need to get your unit moving again. Here's how it works.

Begin by analyzing your team's goals. Do not do this lightly, for it is the basis for all further action. Do not assume that the goals are what they seem to be. What is your business all about? If your goals have been set carefully, this step won't be difficult. But if goal setting has been neglected or attended to rather haphazardly, this will require considerable work.

Carefully examine all projects and activities in the light of your goals. Which ones will help you reach the goals, and which ones won't? Question activities that traditionally have been performed by your team. Where do these activities lead? Do they lead to the *current* goals? Drop anything that won't help. Unfortunately, you may have to cut someone's pet project.

Next, examine all rules and regulations. Which ones facilitate productive results, and which ones hinder them? Unfortunately, rules and regulations often hinder more than they help. Peter Drucker once commented that rules and regulations are more often based on management egos and paranoia than on real reasons. This shouldn't be. A lean company simply can't afford it.

Ask all team members to review their temperament profiles and talents, as they perceive them. Ask them to carefully consider and then list or comment on:

Figure 8-7. Further improved flow process chart for filling out and approving Form X.

FLOW PROCESS CHART									NO. 3 PAGE 1 OF 1

SUMMARY

	PRESENT		PROPOSED		DIFFERENCE	
	NO.	TIME	NO.	TIME	NO.	TIME
○ OPERATIONS	15		4		11	
⇨ TRANSPORTATIONS	2		0		2	
☐ INSPECTIONS	2		0		2	
D DELAYS	5		1		4	
▽ STORAGES	1		1		0	
DISTANCE TRAVELED	600 FT.		0 FT.		600 FT.	

JOB Fill Out and Approve Form X

☐ MAN OR ☑ MATERIAL Form X

CHART BEGINS In A's desk drawer

CHART ENDS In A's out drawer

CHARTED BY AHM DATE

DETAILS OF (Percent Proposed) METHOD	OPERATIONS / TRANSPORT / INSPECTION / DELAY / STORAGE	DISTANCE IN FEET	QUANTITY	TIME	POSSIBILITIES ELIMINATE / COMBINE / CHANGE (STORE / PLACE / PERSON) / IMPROVE	NOTES
1 In A's desk drawer	○⇨☐D▽					
2 Removed and placed on desk	○⇨☐D▽					
3 Filled out and Signed	●⇨☐D▽					Original & 4 copies
4 Carbons and copies separated	○⇨☐D▽					
5 Placed in OUT box	○⇨☐D▽					
6 Waits	○⇨☐D▽					
7	○⇨☐D▽					
8	○⇨☐D▽					
9	○⇨☐D▽					
10	○⇨☐D▽					
11	○⇨☐D▽					
12	○⇨☐D▽					
13	○⇨☐D▽					
14	○⇨☐D▽					
15	○⇨☐D▽					
16	○⇨☐D▽					
17	○⇨☐D▽					
18	○⇨☐D▽					
19	○⇨☐D▽					
20	○⇨☐D▽					
21	○⇨☐D▽					
22	○⇨☐D▽					
23	○⇨☐D▽					
24	○⇨☐D▽					
25	○⇨☐D▽					

- Any special skills they have.
- How their temperament matches the job.
- The pros and cons of the job they currently perform.
- What they like and dislike about their job activities.
- What they believe they contribute most to the team.

You may want to have team members review their colleagues' work, as others can often be more objective in their evaluations. To avoid conflicts or controversy, however, ask people to evaluate only the positive attributes of their team members.

The team leader should do a self-assessment as well as an assessment of each team member. It's also a good idea to encourage team members to assess the team leader.

Identify your team needs on 3×5 cards of one color (for example, white cards). Then identify all the team's talents on 3×5 cards of another color (blue cards, for example). To identify talents accurately, you must integrate your perceptions with those of your team members. Quick judgments may save time, but your conclusions will be more accurate if you discuss individual needs privately with each member.

As you list talents on the blue cards, do not include the names of team members. Put names on the backs of the cards or use a coding system to match talents to people. This prevents stereotyping people and roles.

Sort out the various activities required to accomplish your goals. Match the blue cards to the white cards. Then discuss possible reassignments. Develop your reorganization carefully and discuss new activities with team members individually.

Using the team time/talent assessment has many advantages. First, any misuse of personnel becomes readily apparent. You also see whether or not you'll need additional people, and what kinds of people you should look for. The nature of your retraining needs to meet changing demands also becomes obvious. Team members are considered as individuals, not just as a team component. In the process of trying to match their needs to the team's needs, you enjoy an even greater spirit of teamwork.

> We sometimes try to solve problems by treating the symptoms rather than by identifying the underlying causes.

Change is inevitable. Your team may have to reorganize much more often than it did in the past. Use this exercise as often as necessary to meet changing conditions. It will help your team to get the best from each member and to keep the team pointed in the right direction.

Analyzing Team Time Cost

There's another exercise you can use to facilitate the push for improvement. Most of us respond faster to money than we do to time. Looking at the dollar cost of your team makes good sense. What is the monetary cost of your time to the organization? Many people have never considered the true cost of their time. For those who want to manage their time more effectively, an understanding of what their time is worth is valuable.

The following exercise will enable you to calculate the cost of each team member. By adding together the individual team member costs, you can calculate the total team cost. Individual cost is based on salary plus all the other costs of being employed.

Before starting, make a guess. Think for a moment about how much you and your team members cost your organization. What would you say it costs your employer for one minute of your time? What would you guess the cost is for one minute of your team's time? Now, here' how to get the facts.

	INDIVIDUAL	EXAMPLE
1. *Annual salary.*	1_____	$ 40,000
2. *Fringe benefits.* According to the U.S. Chamber of Commerce, fringe benefits average between 30 and 39 percent of salary costs. If you don't know the exact percent for your organization, use 30 percent.	2_____	12,000

	INDIVIDUAL	EXAMPLE
3. *Total salary plus fringe benefits.*	3_____	$52,000
4. *Overhead*—office space, furniture, telephone, electricity, heat, air conditioning, office machines, cafeterias, building maintenance, office supplies, and so on. For larger organizations, overhead varies from 75 to 100 percent of payroll and fringes. For smaller organizations, overhead may vary from 50 to 75 percent of payroll plus fringes. Unless you know the exact percentage for your organization, use 100 percent of the figure in line 3.	4_____	52,000
5. *Other expenses*—conferences, meetings, company-related travel, educational reimbursement, professional development, entertainment, or other activities reimbursed by your organization.	5_____	3,000
6. *Subtotal.* Add lines 3, 4, and 5. This is your cost to the organization at break-even.	6_____	$107,000
7. *Profit and taxes.* If your organization expects to make a profit, you need to add in your proportion of the profit. Use a figure equal to twice the profit percentage to allow for taxes. For instance, if your firm expects a 10 percent after-tax profit, use 20 percent of the figure shown in line 6.	7_____	21,400

	INDIVIDUAL	EXAMPLE

8. *Total.* Add lines 6 and 7. This is your annual cost to your organization.

   8_____ $128,400

9. *Cost per day.* Divide the figure in line 8 by the number of days you work per year. Most people work 230 days a year. This assumes 52 weekends, 10 holidays, 10 vacation days, and 10 sick days or personal-leave days. If you take a three-week vacation, then you have 225 working days. A four-week vacation would give you 220 working days. On the other hand, a one-week vacation would leave you 235 working days.

   9_____   558

10. *Cost per hour.* Divide the figure in line 9 by the number of hours you normally work in a day. This shows your hourly cost to the organization. (Eight hours are used in the example.) Some people prefer to divide not by the number of total hours on the job but by the number of productive hours on the job. To arrive at productive hours, you need to deduct time for coffee, socializing, waiting, and other nonproductive activities that you engage in each day. Most office personnel report that their productive hours are about 50 to 60 percent of their total hours.

   10a_____   70

	INDIVIDUAL	EXAMPLE
Find the cost per hour of productive time by dividing the figure in line 9 by the number of productive hours in your normal day. Place that amount in line 10b. (Five hours are used in the example.)	10b_____	$112

11. *Cost per minute.* Divide the hourly figure from line 10a or 10b by 60 to find the cost for each minute of your time.

	INDIVIDUAL	EXAMPLE
	11a_____	1.17
	11b_____	1.87

12. *Total team cost per minute.* Add each team member's cost per minute to find the total cost for the team. Our example assumes seven team members.

	EXAMPLE
Person A_____	1.87
Person B_____	1.93
Person C_____	2.56
Person D_____	1.72
Person E_____	2.14
Person F_____	1.99
Person G_____	2.05
Total _____	$14.26

Does the total cost surprise you? Is it higher than you thought it would be? Most of us underestimate true cost. Note that in our example the actual cost is more than three times salary. Most people find that, at a minimum, their true cost is at least two to three times their salary.

Now that you know how much your team time costs, you can use this information in several ways. For instance, you could calculate the total cost of a meeting to decide if it's really worth holding. Or you could use the money value of time to evaluate alternative uses for time.

Many of us do not consider that wasting a few minutes here and there is really serious. But think a moment. If you saw a $10 bill on the floor, would you pick it up or ignore it? In our example, wasting five minutes would cost $71.30. Although that's much more than $10, most people would probably feel worse about the loss of the $10 bill. Think of time as money and you'll learn to internalize its value. As the cliché says, "Money talks!" And rather loudly too.

Return on Time Invested

The Japanese word *kaizen* effectively sums up the rationale for analyzing team time. *Kaizen* means continual incremental improvement. Whatever our time habits are, we didn't get that way overnight. We won't change everything overnight either. The important point is that we *can* change. By continually looking, we will find more and more ways to improve. That's the whole reason for analyzing time.

From a business standpoint, we want to maximize the return on time invested. The techniques discussed in this chapter help you to do that by showing where you can improve. No matter how much time is invested, we want the best return possible. Even if we have large amounts of time available, that does not justify wasting it.

The value of a single minute is critical. A minute is a most revealing time unit. It is often ignored or dismissed as unimportant. We ask others, unthinkingly, to "give us a minute." We eagerly engage in even the most useless activity because "it only takes a minute." We give little thought to being "a few minutes late." Yet minutes are all we have. A new respect for this small time unit might help us become more successful. The way team members put their minutes together determines what results are achieved.

9

Making Meetings
Productive

Ever since we discovered that two heads are better than one, we've been having meetings. Teamwork inevitably means more meetings. We need meetings; you couldn't run even a small operation without them. However, many meetings don't produce much value. The trick is to eliminate the poor ones.

Almost everyone hates to waste time in nonproductive meetings. Yet, year after year, more and more of us go right on wasting still more time in meetings that produce very little. The more time we spend in meetings, the bigger the problem becomes.

Managers can spend 40 to 50 percent of the week in meetings; executives usually average 65 to 75 percent. Both groups report that at least half the meeting time is wasted. A friend of ours recently commented that "managers no longer manage, they only meet." There is, unfortunately, much truth in his observation.

Critiquing Your Meetings

In most organizations, people are never asked whether meetings waste their time. We think asking such a question is an excellent idea. We've asked thousands of people to tell us what causes the meetings they attend to be a waste of time. Here are the most common responses:

- No purpose
- No agenda
- Not sticking to the agenda
- Starting late
- Too long, no time limits
- Not relevant to their work
- Ineffective meeting leader
- Poor participation
- A few people dominate the meeting
- People not prepared
- No decisions or conclusions
- No follow-up
- Redundant, rambling discussion
- Actions already determined before the meeting
- Hidden agendas introduced
- Side issues discussed
- Key people missing
- Too many people at the meeting
- Wrong people present
- Short notice or lead time
- Not knowing what is expected
- Too many interruptions

This list illustrates a lot of dissatisfaction with meetings. Not only do people usually keep these feelings bottled up, but their negative attitudes affect other areas of their work as well.

Negative experiences with meetings are a major deterrent to team time management. Past experience with poor meetings leads to lowered expectations about future meetings. If you want to promote team time management, you must make your meetings excellent.

If you have a problem with meetings, here is a technique that can quickly help you to improve meeting quality. First, survey everyone. Ask people to write down all the things that cause meetings to waste their time. Do this anonymously. Our research shows that almost no one is ever asked this question.

Next, list all the responses and look for frequently mentioned responses. You will probably notice that some items appear again and again. When we surveyed 160 supervisors in one company, we received 58 different responses. However, fourteen items were on 87 percent of the lists.

Take most frequently mentioned responses and create a checklist. On the checklist, pose each item as a question requiring a yes or no answer. For example, here's how we turned fourteen frequent complaints into questions:

1. Did you clearly understand the purpose of this meeting?   Yes   No
2. Did you have at least two days' notice of this meeting?   Yes   No
3. Was there an agenda for the meeting?   Yes   No
4. Was this meeting relevant to your job?   Yes   No
5. Did the meeting start on time?   Yes   No
6. Was the meeting interrupted?   Yes   No
7. Were you prepared for this meeting?   Yes   No
8. Did the meeting stick to the agenda?   Yes   No
9. Was there adequate participation?   Yes   No
10. Did the meeting last too long?   Yes   No
11. Were the right people present?   Yes   No
12. Was appropriate action taken?   Yes   No
13. Did the leader control the meeting well?   Yes   No
14. Were the meeting goals reached?   Yes   No

Give everyone a supply of these checklists. Then, at the end of each meeting, ask people to complete the critique checklist and leave it in a box. No names, just responses. If you're the person in charge, this provides you with instant feedback about the quality of the meeting. You'll know just what to fix to improve future meetings.

This approach has several advantages. It is specific to your team. It provides instant, precise feedback. It is anonymous and allows people to be candid. It is simple and easy to use.

> An effective meeting is one that achieves its purpose.

Clarifying the Purpose of Meetings

Simply stated, an effective meeting is one that achieves its purpose. The worst thing you can do is to call a meeting without knowing what you intend to accomplish. Meeting for the sake of meeting or just because a meeting is on the calendar is usually a waste of time.

Ask yourself what you expect to accomplish. What result do you hope to achieve by the end of the meeting? Discourage and discontinue unnecessary meetings. If you can't think of a good reason to meet, don't. This may not always be easy, because many meetings have become institutionalized over the years. We meet every week simply because it's the Weekly Meeting. We have frequent team meetings because someone said it would help "improve communications."

Learn to make decisions without meetings. Never involve the whole group if you can do something better on an individual basis. Think things through before automatically calling a meeting. Could you achieve the same result some other way? Does the problem deserve a meeting? Is there an alternative?

Use some kind of meeting planner, like the one shown in Figure 9-1, to think through your intended meeting. Asking the questions on the form forces you to think about the potential value of the meeting. If it still seems like a good idea to hold one, the form will also help you to use everyone's time productively.

There are often other options besides meetings. For instance, when one-way communications are appropriate, they can be handled by memos, voice-mail, electronic mail, or fax. Telephone conferences can be just as effective as face-to-face meetings.

You might also ask yourself if a meeting is worth the cost? Chapter 8 tells you how to calculate the cost of your time. Add up the cost per minute for each person who will be attending, multiplied by the total time assigned the meeting. Listen to

Figure 9-1. Sample meeting planner.

Meeting Planner

PURPOSE: What should the meeting accomplish?

PEOPLE: Who should come, what will they contribute?

PLAN: Agenda topics, sequence, intended results, time needed, resources or materials needed

PLACE: Location, date, starting time, ending time, directions, logistics

how money talks. Do you expect the meeting to produce at least as much value as its cost? If the answer is no, don't hold the meeting.

Considering Which People to Invite

Choose your participants carefully. If you include too many people, or people who don't actually have to be there, you'll have a tougher time getting anything accomplished. Invite only those whose attendance is necessary. Extra people create added confusion and increase the likelihood that your agenda will go astray. Be certain that key decision makers are present; if they can't be, you should probably postpone the meeting.

Try to keep the total number down. Five to eight people is an ideal size for action meetings. Studies show that when group size rises above eight, it is harder to reach decisions. A meeting of two dozen people often fizzles out, with no action taken. Potential interactions are a function of the number of people attending: $I = n(n-1)$. Figure 9-2 shows how the potential number of interactions escalates rapidly with even a small increase in the number of people attending. With three people, the interaction potential is only 6; with four people, the potential interactions rise to 12; with ten people, the potential interactions jump to 90. The more people attending, the slower the meeting becomes. The sheer volume of interactions between people guarantees it.

To help reduce overall meeting size, consider part-time attendance. Allow people to come when they're needed and then to leave once they've made their contribution. There is no point in having people sit all the way through a meeting if only part of it is relevant to them.

Be certain that everyone knows what is expected of them.

Figure 9-2. Interaction growth rates.

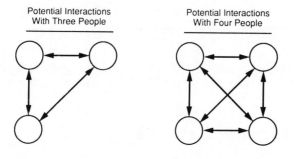

Potential Interactions
With Three People

Potential Interactions
With Four People

Tell them what to bring to the meeting. Suggest visual aids that will help them to make their points faster and better. Give them enough advance notice so they can be properly prepared.

The Mechanics of Planning and Holding Meetings

Making Good Agendas

Whenever you must hold a meeting, be sure to have a prepared agenda. And if possible, prepare the agenda ahead of time. Invite meeting participants to contribute agenda items. Then distribute it early so that everyone has time to prepare properly.

The agenda should indicate the purpose of each topic and the direction of the discussion. It should include the intended results, actions, or decisions expected. You might also want to specify the amount of time you plan to devote to each agenda item. This assures that the most important items get the most time. It also helps keep the meeting on schedule.

Designate the people who will be called upon to discuss certain points. Tell these people how detailed you expect their contribution to be. This approach allows you to delegate responsibility for the meeting to others. It also allows them to bring their best ideas to the meeting.

You may even want to make your expectations public. When you prepare your agenda, note the people who will be presenting. Everyone will realize that these individuals should be prepared for a good presentation.

A well-prepared agenda helps you to stay on course and to resist people who go off on tangents. In any group there are always people who would rather talk about anything except the business at hand. The agenda is like a roadmap that instantly tells you when the group is straying off course.

A good agenda form, like the one in Figure 9-3, can help you prepare excellent agendas. Notice how it covers all the points we have just discussed.

Figure 9-3.   Sample meeting agenda.

Meeting Agenda

Date	Time	Location

Purpose of Meeting

TOPIC	TIME	PRESENTER

Objective - Intended Result	Decisions - Comments - Follow-Up Actions

TOPIC	TIME	PRESENTER

Objective - Intended Result	Decisions - Comments - Follow-Up Actions

TOPIC	TIME	PRESENTER

Objective - Intended Result	Decisions - Comments - Follow-Up Actions

Setting Time Limits

Most meetings could achieve their intended results in less time. So set a time limit and stick to it. It's often a good idea to note the time allotment directly on the agenda. That puts everyone on notice. Allow adequate time, but not too much. Remember, though, that short meetings are not necessarily better meetings. The key is to allow just the amount of time needed to reach the objective.

One effective way to shorten meeting time is to hold stand-up meetings. It may surprise you how much can be done in 15 to 20 minutes. Some companies have even built stand-up conference tables to facilitate handling papers at these meetings.

Don't make people too comfortable during the meeting. In other words, don't give people two-hour chairs if you intend to keep them only 30 minutes. The length of a meeting is often directly related to the comfort of the chairs and the amount of coffee available.

Consider the best time to schedule the meeting. Don't combine meetings and meals. That combination takes more time and is often less effective. Setting a meeting just before lunch or just before quitting time is a good way to assure stopping on time. People work a little harder and faster when it's almost time to eat or to go home.

Starting on Time

No matter what meeting you attend, someone is always late. Everyone sits around waiting for the laggards to show up. Or you stop the meeting to bring them up to date when they do finally arrive. If six people wait 10 minutes, the company has lost one hour. That is nonproductive, wasted time.

Many companies fine people who show up late. They use the money collected from tardy members for parties, donate it to charity, or simply treat it as miscellaneous income. Other companies look for ways to reward those who are early or on time rather than penalize latecomers directly.

Some companies lock the door when it is time to start the meeting. Some remove all empty chairs from the room, forcing latecomers to stand.

Some people arrange the agenda so that items of interest to habitual latecomers appear first. In other cases, the late arrivals get the most undesirable assignments.

Some people indirectly emphasize timing by setting unusual starting times. For example, instead of starting at 9:00 A.M., you set the meeting to begin at 8:57 or 9:03. This both focuses people on the time and subtly says that minutes count and you expect to run on time.

Probably the simplest and most effective method is just to start on time. Don't lightly excuse or condone lateness. Don't be accommodating to latecomers. Above all, don't reward lateness. If you delay a meeting by waiting for stragglers, you guarantee that people will be late in the future. They may even plan on being tardy, for experience has shown that your meetings never start on time.

Following Up on Meetings

Keep concise notes at the meeting. These minutes can be an important time-saving tool. It is usually best to assign the note-taking duties to a secretary rather than to one of the participants. Minutes should also be distributed within 24 hours. Minutes distributed more than a day after the event lose their effectiveness. Besides, the longer the delay, the less people will remember. Even if there are errors in the minutes, they may pass unnoticed.

Be sure to note the names of people responsible for follow-up actions. Indicate the due dates and time frames and mention whom they should contact if they run into problems. A form like the one shown in Figure 9-4 makes this easy to do.

Check at appropriate times after the meeting to make sure that things are progressing as they should. Unfortunately, many meetings turn into repeat sessions because one or more people didn't do what they were supposed to do after the last meeting.

Stimulating Positive Discussion

The success of any discussion depends on the level and quality of participation. Some people hardly need an invitation to jump right in, while others have to be dragged into the discussion. Asking questions is one of the best ways to make sure everyone gets into the act.

There are generally four kinds of questions: (1) general questions, which call for a broad range of potential responses; (2) specific questions, which focus on one particular aspect of

Figure 9-4. Meeting follow-up.

Meeting Follow-Up

WHO Person receiving the assignment	WHAT Nature of the assignment	WHEN Due date for assignment

the discussion; (3) overhead questions, which are thrown out to the group so that someone can volunteer a response; and (4) direct questions, which are directed to a specific person for response.

Because general and overhead questions are less threatening, they may be a good way to start. But they can also be ineffective if no one volunteers a response. Direct and specific questions, which are the most effective, also require the greatest amount of comfort and trust within the group. These two types of questions are particularly useful for making sure that all viewpoints and all people are included in the discussion.

In addition to asking questions, there are several other ways to help make your discussion periods more productive:

- *Use paraphrasing to make sure people are listening to one another.* You can both do this yourself and ask others to do it as well.
- *Ask people for their feelings and opinions, not just for factual information.* Feelings are sometimes more important than facts. It often helps if the team leader shares his or her feelings first.
- *Ask people to clarify or expand their comments.* If you don't understand, someone else is probably having difficulty too. Asking for examples or analogies is a good way to help people clarify their thoughts.
- *Go for consensus whenever you can.* It is usually better than asking for a vote, though sometimes asking for a show of hands allows you to see quickly where things stand on a particular point.
- *Be sure to take breaks.* You should allow a break at least every 45 to 60 minutes for most groups.
- *Go around the table and ask for everyone's comments.* Ask for specifics. Don't settle for vague, ambiguous comments.
- *Be supportive of each individual.* Don't criticize or make fun of anyone. You never make a mistake by boosting someone's self-esteem.
- *Confront differences.* There's no point in ignoring them or pretending they don't exist. But remember to disagree without being disagreeable.
- *Question assumptions, even ones that are only implied.* Our assumptions often limit our possibilities. Change the assumptions, and new possibilities surface. It also helps to check out assumptions because they are often wrong.
- *Ask for action ideas on how to get started.*

Handling Problem People

By now, you're certainly aware that people come in all sizes and flavors. Temperament alone accounts for that. But even beyond temperament, we all have pluses and minuses. This is especially true when we get together for a meeting. An effective meeting leader must learn how to draw on the strengths of each participant while avoiding the weaknesses.

Margie Wood is a consultant friend in New York who has years of experience in helping people improve their facilitation skills. She graciously shared her perceptions of several common types of people who come to meetings and of what you can do to draw out their strengths and avoid their weaknesses.

- *Quarrelers.* Some people are quarrelsome. They seem to thrive on arguments and pick fights with everyone. Keep calm and don't get involved with them. Your challenge is to keep them from monopolizing the meeting. Sometimes, you may have to be direct and firm.
- *Positives.* They can be counted on to see the bright side of things. They're a great help in a discussion and you'd love to have a lot of them at most meetings. Call on them frequently, and let their contributions add up.
- *Know-it-alls.* No matter what the topic, this person knows everything there is to know . . . or at least thinks he does. The group soon tires of his expertise, and will keep him in check. Let them do so, but keep it as humane as possible. Sometimes this person really does have a wealth of knowledge.
- *Talkers.* These people ramble on and on, whether or not they have anything useful to contribute. Limit their speaking time, interrupting them if necessary.
- *Wallflowers.* These folks almost never volunteer any comments. You have to draw them out. Ask them direct questions, but don't embarrass them. Boost their self-confidence, and give them credit for their contributions.
- *Trappers.* This person tries hard to trap the leader. Don't fall into it. Pass her persistent questions back to the group and let others respond.
- *Highbrows.* They're always above the rest of us. Don't criticize them. Agree with them, and use the "yes, but . . ." technique.
- *Negatives.* No matter what it is, they're against it. Don't

succumb to frustration. Listen to them, and draw on their knowledge whenever it is appropriate. Unfortunately, they often do see real problems that many of us overlook. Try to balance them with your positives so that they don't swamp the meeting.

Participating Effectively

As we've emphasized with every aspect of team time management, the quality of a meeting is not the sole responsibility of the person in charge. Whenever meetings become major time-wasters, you usually discover that meeting attenders are also at fault.

Everyone should ask questions before the meeting. What do you plan to accomplish at this meeting? Why do you need me? What do you expect me to contribute? How long will the meeting take? May I come when you need me and leave when my part is over? Use questions as a way to encourage and influence good meeting preparation.

Ask questions during the meeting. How does this discussion apply to our purpose? Can we get back to the agenda? Shouldn't this point be taken up at a different time?

Ask questions of yourself. Am I really prepared? Do I contribute to the side-chatter and wander off the agenda? Am I the kind of participant I would want others to be if I were leading this meeting?

Asking questions helps in two ways. First, it encourages the person in charge to do a thorough planning job ahead of time. Second, it helps reduce the time you waste in nonproductive meetings.

Make a list of your most frequent reactions as you take part in meetings. Your feelings are probably shared by others. Remember that your choices with respect to improving a meeting are the same as those in other areas of your life: You can change it, leave it, or drop it.

A person can breathe new life into meetings simply by changing his or her own behavior. After analyzing your own behavior, consciously respond in a different way. If you are usually silent, make an effort to voice your opinion. If you are usually outspoken, sit back and quietly observe what is taking place.

Many people complain that they have no influence over improving meetings, but this is simply not true. If all participants requested improvements, very few meeting leaders would be able to resist those requests. It is precisely because participants accept ineffective meetings that they continue.

Making Good Presentations

A big problem with many meetings is that people take forever to get to the point. They try to include too many details, and their points are disorganized. The audience becomes frustrated.

Several years ago, our friend Frank Hardesty showed us an approach he called SOPPADA, which can help you make great presentations quickly.* SOPPADA is an acronym for:

S – Subject
O – Objective
P – Present situation
P – Proposal
A – Advantages
D – Disadvantages
A – Action

According to Frank, SOPPADA works because it puts your thoughts into a creatively chronological order. It won't make you any smarter, but it does help you bring your full intelligence to bear. The difficulty is that our ideas are often a mishmash of good reasoning and faulty reasoning. We have a bunch of good points and bad points, some objective, some subjective, all thrown together with bits and pieces of logic here and there. If presented, the whole idea would probably

*T. Frank Hardesty and W. Wayne Scott, *Action Tools for Increasing Individual Management Productivity* (Pittsburgh, Penna.: Westinghouse Learning Corporation, 1976).

collapse under the weight of its complexity and disorganization. And that's where SOPPADA comes in.

As shown in Figure 9-5, preparing and following a SOP-PADA sheet will keep you on target. The *subject* sets the stage, and the *objective* lays out the goals to be achieved. The *present situation,* in brief compass, describes what's happening now and why that is unacceptable. The word *problem* never appears;

Figure 9-5. SOPPADA sheet.

Here's My Idea!

Subject:

Objective:

Present Situation:

Proposal:

Advantages:
1.
2.
3.

Disadvantages:
1.
2.

Action:

it isn't necessary. By stating the objective and the present situation, you define the problem. Quickly and neatly.

The *proposal* lays out the steps you'd like to take to create a better condition or improve the present situation. Once you've narrowed your thinking through stating the objective and present situation, the proposal almost defines itself. Some people are tempted to stop at this point. Don't do it. You're not yet ready for the pressure of public discussion.

Every proposal has *advantages*. These are the benefits that can be expected from acting on the proposal. The temptation is to write down too many advantages, to oversell your proposal. Include the three best advantages. If there are more than three advantages, save the others and use them during the discussion.

Every proposal also has *disadvantages*, even though we may not like to admit it. If you don't point out the disadvantages, someone else will. When someone else does this, your proposal is automatically weakened. When you bring them up yourself, the proposal appears objectively balanced.

Although you included three advantages, mention only two disadvantages. Be sure they are the two biggest disadvantages you can think of. If you can't think of any disadvantages, remember that every idea has at least two: It involves a change, and it will probably cost something.

Descriptions of disadvantages contain two sentences. The first sentence describes the disadvantage. The second sentence begins with the word *however* and then goes on to tell how the disadvantage can be overcome. This takes the sting out of the disadvantage.

Finally, you describe the first step you plan to take when your idea is accepted. This shows that you have thought things through and are prepared to implement the idea.

SOPPADA is easy and fun to use. It helps you present your ideas simply, quickly, clearly, and objectively. What's even better, your ideas are more likely to be accepted when you use this approach.

Meetings are the lifeline of team time management.

Good meetings don't just happen. They must be carefully planned and executed. Just because people are put in leadership positions doesn't mean that they automatically know how to plan and run meetings well. Buy them books. Show them good videotapes. Hold training sessions.

Of all the major timewasters, bad meetings are probably the easiest to eradicate. And eliminating wasted time in meetings will probably do more good for more people at one time than solving any other time problem. It takes a little effort, but the rewards are especially attractive.

Meetings are the lifeline of team time management. Just because they are important, however, doesn't mean that you should have more of them. You probably don't need more meetings, just more effective meetings. Almost everyone will welcome meetings that are more effective and take less time. When you meetings are productive, they become valuable for everyone instead of simply timewasters. At this point, team members will look forward to them as an important time for sharing ideas and making progress.

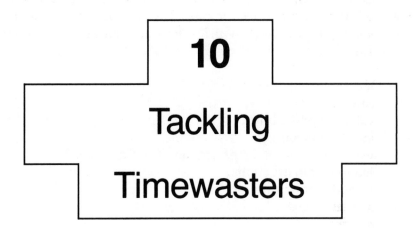

10

Tackling

Timewasters

After more than twenty years of working with time management, we've reached one inescapable conclusion: We all create time problems for the people we work with. For effective team time management, we must work at reducing these problems.

For starters, it might help if you asked your teammates this shocking question: How do I waste your time and hinder your performance? If you've never asked this question before, don't expect any miracles. The first time you ask, you are likely to raise their anxiety level. They'll be wondering what you're up to and whether or not they can trust you with this kind of information. Don't worry about it, just keep asking the question. Sooner or later, they'll begin responding.

If you're sincerely interested in their responses and keep asking the question, people will eventually risk a response. Be careful how you handle it. The best way is just to listen, thank them for their comments, and then fix anything you can. If, on the other hand, you attack them, aggressively defend yourself, or deny the validity of their statements, they'll stop talking to you. Bite your tongue if necessary and listen to what they have to say.

Whenever we conduct time management seminars in companies, we always send people a questionnaire before the seminar. One of our questions is, "How could you save time for the people you work with?" Here are the most frequent responses:

"Get better organized."
"Interrupt them less."
"Improve procedures."
"Improve meetings."
"Give them complete information the first time."
"Give clear instructions."
"Provide more training."
"Respond faster."

You might start a dialogue going in your team with the same question. After asking for anonymous responses, collect them, tabulate them, and discuss the results. You'll probably notice two things. First, the actions cited that would save time for others will help you too. Second, it would not cost anything to do most of these things. In fact, it makes you wonder why you aren't already doing them. As Will Rogers used to say, "If we did half of what we know we should do, we'd be twice as well off as we are."

Take your time when you deliver crucial messages. People frequently complain that they are given instructions too quickly and do not have time to absorb them. Being afraid to appear "slow," they often say that they understand—but then perform with a poor knowledge of what they should be doing. Take the time to give instructions carefully, particularly on new and unfamiliar projects.

When you are giving instructions, remember that concepts familiar to you may not be familiar to others. Wouldn't you be confused if someone told you to "get the SWP report to Sam's office" when you had never heard of SWP or Sam? Take the time to carefully define your terms at the outset in order to save yourself and others a lot of heartache later.

One way to guard against miscommunication is to restate your idea in a variety of ways until you are certain it has been clearly understood. You may want to ask other people to repeat what you have said in order to confirm that they understand. It is also a good idea to follow up your verbal message with a brief note restating the gist of your instructions.

Developing the On-Time Habit

Planning and coordinating activities with your team members will reduce conflicts and bottlenecks. You will all spend less time waiting for each other. But that's only the beginning point in reducing waiting time. Some waiting is inevitable and unavoidable. Just accept it and learn to live with it. But much wasteful waiting could be trimmed if we all adopted the on-time habit. Show up for meetings and appointments on time. Deliver work on time. When people have appointments to see you, receive them on time. B. C. Forbes, the founder of *Forbes Magazine*, said he never quite trusted the person who was late. Lots of people feel the same way, although they may not say so. Being late definitely works against you.

Waiting is part of any job. We wait for people who are late for meetings and appointments. We wait for work that is overdue but incomplete. We wait for decisions, or approvals, or information we need. But waiting wastes time, delays results, and destroys relationships.

Being late occasionally is inevitable, but being late regularly isn't. Why are many people always late? Psychologists have pointed out several possible reasons for persistent tardiness:

> *Rebellion.* By being late, some people secretly feel that they're beating a system that prizes efficiency and time consciousness. Many people aren't even aware that they are doing this.
>
> *Exaggerated sense of self-importance.* Coming late may be a person's way of saying, "I'm a busy person, which means I'm important." Or, it may be the latecomer's attempt to convey the thought that he is more important than the others involved.
>
> *Perfectionism compulsion.* People may be unable to leave one

task until it's done to their satisfaction. This perfection-ism sometimes causes them to be late for work and late in going home.

Uncertainty and fear. People are sometimes late because they're afraid of what will happen to them when they arrive, even though the situation may be no more threat-ening than the usual interaction between themselves and someone they don't particularly like.

Desire for attention. Some people like to be the focus of attention. If they arrive on time, no one will notice them. Others may even take their promptness for granted.

Manipulation. Time is a precious commodity and can be a powerful weapon. Being late is one way to manipulate a situation. It can convey the idea of superiority, anger, or revenge.

Occasionally people are late because "things happen"; however, things seem to happen more often to some people than to others. In Chapters 3, 4, and 5, we discussed the different temperaments. The Time Teaser personality often has trouble being on time and must make a real effort to overcome this tendency. If you're a Time Teaser, or just frequently late, you may want to try some of these ideas to help you break your tardiness habit.

• *Keep a time log for a week.* Note the actual time you arrived at appointments as opposed to the time you were scheduled to arrive. Analyze your log. How many times were you late? What were the consequences to you and to others? What was your excuse to yourself and to others?

• *Begin planning your day.* Many habitually tardy people are poor planners. Lack of planning is a major part of their prob-lems. If you have a tardiness problem, try working backwards from your appointments. For example, if you must be at work at 9 A.M., plan to arrive at 8:50. Decide the real amount of travel time required to arrive at 8:50, how long it takes you to get up, eat breakfast, read the paper, shower, and dress. Set the alarm for when you *must* get up.

▪ *Set your watch early.* Vince Lombardi, legendary coach of the Green Bay Packers football team, told his players that if they weren't 15 minutes early, they were late. Players set their watches ahead to make sure they were on time.

▪ *Focus on your leaving time, not the arrival time.* Suppose you must be at a meeting by 2:00 P.M. If you focus on leaving at 1:40 P.M., instead of arriving at 2:00, you're more likely to arrive on time.

▪ *Estimate your time needs.* How long will it actually take to complete an action? Running out of time often results from not considering how much time you really needed in the first place.

▪ *Start on time.* Don't wait until the last minute. Give yourself plenty of time to do the job right and still finish by the deadline.

▪ *Avoid the "one last thing" tendency.* When it's time to go, leave. Don't give in to the temptation to take one more call, handle one more question, or write one more memo. Trying to squeeze in one more task will often make you late.

▪ *Allow for the unexpected.* Things frequently go wrong. When you're in a hurry, more things go wrong. Allow extra time in your schedule to handle unexpected problems. Even with a good plan, things won't always go smoothly. A last-minute phone call from an important client can still make you late for the next event. But if you build in safety margins, you'll find that the unexpected doesn't upset your schedule so often.

▪ *Check out your environment.* Does it hinder you from being punctual? Could you better arrange some things at home to enable you to get ready faster? Would the drive to work be less congested if you left 15 minutes earlier?

▪ *Ask for help.* Are you trying to do so much that you never really have enough time for anything? If you routinely drop your kids off at school on the way to work, perhaps your spouse or a neighbor who goes that way could help you.

▪ *Reward yourself when you're on time.* People who arrive a little early already have the reward of feeling "together" rather than frazzled. You can also reward yourself by slipping in a little thinking or reading time.

We each have a responsibility to ourselves and to others. Living and working together seem to go better when things happen on time. The mature team time manager develops the habit of punctuality. And being on time is almost always considered a good habit by others.

Analyzing Team Timewasters

We waste a lot of each other's time, consciously or otherwise. The unfortunate part is that we don't stop very often to think about what we're doing to each other, nor do we talk about time problems very often. Mostly we just complain, and nothing changes.

Teams exhibit complex, dynamic behavior patterns. Because of their constant interactions, team members often create time problems for each other. Many of these time problems could be easily resolved if team members just talked about them. The trick is to discuss them without pointing blame at anyone. When others blame us, we tend to get defensive, which makes improvement less likely.

Preparing a team timewaster profile can be a good way to start a positive dialogue. This analysis provides a common base for action. It can also be the catalyst that inspires team members to encourage and support each other in trying to improve.

This analysis exercise is based on the nineteen activities most often mentioned as timewasters. It is easy to do and takes very little time. There are only five steps involved.

1. Give each team member a copy of the timewaster list. Ask each person to select the top six timewasters from the list and then to indicate their rank order, with No. 1 representing the top timewaster.

2. Assign each person's six timewasters the following weights:

No. 1 timewaster = 30
No. 2 timewaster = 25
No. 3 timewaster = 20

No. 4 timewaster = 15
No. 5 timewaster = 10
No. 6 timewaster = 5

3. Record the rank and weights for the timewasters identified by each team member on your profile sheet, a sample of which is shown in Figure 10-1. The nineteen timewasters are listed down the rows on the left-hand side. The columns reflect each person's rank orderings and weights.

4. Add the weights across all columns for each timewaster identified. Record the total team weights in the "Combined Weight" column.

5. Determine the final ranking for the team timewasters. The timewaster with the greatest combined weight becomes the No. 1 timewaster for the team. Continue in this fashion until you have identified the top six timewasters for the team.

With this procedure, you can identify both individual timewasters and timewasters that are shared by the team. When finished, the profile provides an excellent basis for team discussion about the causes of and possible solutions to each timewaster.

You might begin the discussion by looking at the final list and saying, "Here is the final list of major timewasters for this team. Because interruptions are No. 1, let's talk about how we might minimize them." That can lead to a brainstorming session that will probably produce many suggestions. Some of the suggestions are bound to work. Team members simply decide which ones they want to try first and then act to implement them.

Whenever you discuss time problems with your team, try to do it without pinning the blame on anyone. In a nonthreatening atmosphere, people generally discuss time waste openly. Such a discussion quickly produces ideas about how timewasters might be eliminated or reduced. At this point, you have the beginning of a team action plan.

The team timewaster profile can also be valuable in discussing the good use of time. In other words, if some wasted

Figure 10-1.   Team timewaster profile.

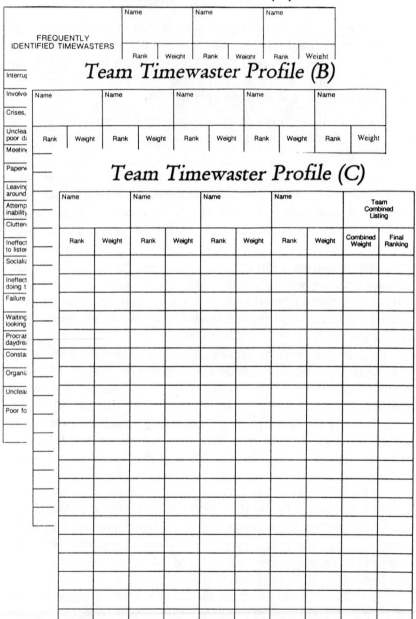

Team Timewaster Profile (A)

FREQUENTLY IDENTIFIED TIMEWASTERS	Name		Name		Name	
	Rank	Weight	Rank	Weight	Rank	Weight

Team Timewaster Profile (B)

Name		Name		Name		Name		Name	
Rank	Weight	Rank	Weight	Rank	Weight	Rank	Weight	Rank	Weight

Team Timewaster Profile (C)

Name		Name		Name		Name		Team Combined Listing	
Rank	Weight	Rank	Weight	Rank	Weight	Rank	Weight	Combined Weight	Final Ranking

time can be recovered, how should it be spent? The discussion should emphasize intended results and planning. When you focus on plans for accomplishing objectives, you discover ways in which everyone can use time more effectively. That's what you're after.

Your discussions may produce differences of opinion about cause-and-effect relationships. We sometimes try to solve problems by treating the symptoms rather than by identifying their underlying causes. As a result, our perceptions are often fuzzy as to what truly causes a particular effect. The solution to these disagreements is to dig a little deeper before jumping to conclusions. You might want to go back and review the discussion on facts versus inferences in Chapter 6. The first thought is not always the best thought. The real problem and the specific objective should be identified before any attempt is made to resolve differences of opinions about causes and effects.

Charles Kepner and Benjamin Tregoe prescribe a systematic analysis to specify what the problem is before looking for its possible causes.* They define a problem as a deviation from a standard, as something that should not be. They suggest asking the normal what-where-when-how questions, but add a unique twist. To make the problem description truly precise, you must separate what the problem *is* from what it *is not*. We have found this particularly helpful when trying to nail down elusive issues. Describe where it is happening, as well as where it is not. Describe what is happening, as well as what is not happening. Describe when it happens, as well as when it does not. Once the deviation, or problem, has been defined precisely, you can proceed to look for probable causes that fit both the *is* and the *is not* conditions.

Socrates wrote that the unexamined life is not worth living. The implication is that taking the time to examine yourself can improve the quality of your life. We believe that the same point can be made about many of the timewasters we face as team members. By examining ourselves and each other, we can solve many of our problems.

---

*Charles H. Kepner and Benjamin B. Tregoe, *The Rational Manager* (Princeton, N.J.: Kepner-Tregoe, Inc., 1965).

"If we did half of what we know we should do,
we'd be twice as well off as we are."

Think about each of your team members, the people you spend the most time with. How do you waste their time? How do they waste yours? Write your thoughts down. Use something like the timewaster analysis sheet shown in Figure 10-2. For each problem you see, what are the possible solutions?

Good time management requires effective teamwork. Each of us must use our own time well, and we must also help others to use their time to advantage. Invest some of your time in analyzing your time relationships with others. Discuss the results with those concerned and seek solutions that will benefit all of you.

Handling Interruptions

"Hi there! Gotta minute?" How many times have you heard this? Trouble is, this "minute" is likely to last at least 20 minutes. Whether they're telephone calls or drop-in visitors, interruptions are probably one of the major timewasters facing your team. They often take up a sizable portion of the day. In an office, for example, you can count on being interrupted every 6 to 8 minutes. Some interruptions are positive, others are negative. Some are worthwhile, others worthless. Some are controllable, others aren't. But all of them cut down on the time you have for working on things you consider important.

The first thing to realize is that interruptions are part of the job, and it may be your attitude that needs adjusting. When interrupted, most of us are at least mildly irritated; we don't like to stop what we're doing to focus on something else. Try to look at the interruption in a different way. Instead of being upset when an interruption occurs, think of it simply as part of your job. You'll be less frustrated and better able to stay in control of the situation.

Realize, too, that you will never achieve total control over interruptions. When you work with people, you must resign

Figure 10-2. Team timewaster analysis.

Team Timewaster Analysis

List each of your team members. Think carefully about how you waste their time, and how they waste your time.
Consider how these conditions could be changed. Share your ideas with each other, and act on them right away.

Team Member	How do I waste this person's time, and hinder their performance?	How does this person waste my time and hinder my performance?

yourself to their unpredictable behavior. The basic idea is to control the controllable but to accept the noncontrollable. The key is to allow enough time in your schedule to deal with these unexpected, uncontrollable events. If you give yourself some flexibility, you won't be so frustrated when interruptions occur. If you don't allow adequate flexibility in your schedule, the interruptions will occur anyway, and your frustrations will soar.

Analyzing Interruptions

Unfortunately, most people do nothing but complain about their interruption problems. Only a few systematically analyze them and work to eliminate, reduce, or control them. Even a little constructive action is better than years of complaining.

The single most useful approach to reducing interruptions is to keep records. Note who interrupts you, when they interrupt, how long the interruption takes, and what it is about. By studying this record you can learn a great deal about your interruption patterns.

Chances are, you will find that most of your interruptions come from those who are closest to you. These are the people who talk to you most often—your team members. Your records will probably show that most of the contacts concern routine or trivial matters. Only a few are critically important.

Look for patterns among your interruptions. Are there a few people who interrupt you constantly? Do some issues generate far more interruptions than others? Are telephone calls a bigger problem than drop-in visitors? Are mornings better or worse than afternoons? How many of the calls you receive are to the wrong number? How many interruptions concern social matters instead of work? No matter what the pattern, knowing what it is puts you way ahead. You can't solve a problem until you have accurately identified it.

Everyone struggles with interruptions. Most of us constantly complain about them. It would be far better to analyze them, then work systematically to reduce them. In the words of my first boss, who was somewhat of a philosopher, "It is better to light one candle than to curse the darkness."

Keeping It Brief

If you can't prevent all interruptions, you can nevertheless often control how long they last. If you can keep them short, you have solved at least half the problem.

For example, an AT&T study in 1989 reported that the average unplanned telephone call takes almost 11 minutes. In contrast, the average planned call lasts only about 7 minutes. Planning telephone calls would obviously help both parties.

Consider how to greet callers. "Hi, Tom! How are you?" is an open invitation to visit. Your caller might even feel obliged to respond with small talk. However, the caller is more likely to get right to the point if you say, "Hi, Tom! How can I help you?"

Reorganize your work or the timing of your tasks. For instance, most people go to lunch at the same time: 12:00 noon. If you were to work during the normal lunch hour, you would probably have very few interruptions. Another possibility is the first hour of the day. Try to concentrate on your important work while most people are occupied with coffee, conversation, and newspapers. Most interruption patterns don't build up until after 9:00 or 9:30 A.M.

Tell visitors you have only a few minutes. Gently encourage them to get to the point quickly. Keep a large clock close by and glance at it from time to time. Or use a timer to remind you to keep conversations short. The more people are aware of time, the less time they waste.

Train people to do their thinking before they come talk to you. Ask them to write down exactly what they want you to do. Frequently, they will solve their own problems when they are forced to think about them. At the very least, your time together will be shorter and more productive when they have prepared first.

Go to other people's offices when they need to see you. It makes them feel good, and gives you more control. It's usually easier to leave someone else's office than it is to get them out of your office.

Finally, be creative. Several years ago, a client showed us an excellent example of how to keep interruptions short. He had two inches cut off the front legs of his visitors' chairs.

Standing Up

When someone drops in to see you, don't remain sitting at your desk. Stand up, look your visitor in the eye, and ask,

"How can I help you?" Unless the visit requires sitting, remain standing while you talk.

Most of us sit when we go to talk with others. Think about it. What might happen if you stood up when someone dropped in to see you? If you don't sit down, your visitor probably won't sit either. It would be a breech of good etiquette. Instead, your interrupter will probably get to the point quicker and be on his way sooner. Then, you can sit down and get back to your own work.

Standing might even improve your relationships with others. Here is a common example. Someone pops into your office. You don't stop writing or even lift your eyes from whatever you are doing. Yet, you tell her to go ahead, you are listening. Do you ever think about the message you have just sent to that person? If you stood up when she entered, you would automatically give her your full attention. The nonverbal message you send would be much more positive, and you would save time in the bargain.

Bunching Things Together

Most of us interrupt others in a haphazard manner. We phone them or drop in on them whenever it suits us. By and large, our focus is on what *we* are doing, what *we* need, and what *we* are trying to avoid. We seldom stop to think about what this constant barrage does to others—though we often complain about what their constant interruptions do to *us.*

Some of our interruptions are important, but let's face it, most are merely routine. Timing is not critical for most routine matters. They need doing, but it doesn't have to be right now. Therefore, we could bunch several of these routine matters together and handle them all at one time.

You may find that the fast pace of your job helps create constant interruptions. For example, suppose your job involves many projects. You are in and out of the office throughout the week. People never know for sure when they can count on seeing you. Even when you are in, you're always busy. So, they begin to catch you whenever they can. Every time they think of something, they call you or pop into your office. After a while, this becomes their regular modus operandi.

To get better results, ask people to hold their routine items so you can go over them all at one time. You bunch your routine items too. Schedule regular meetings with key people. Encourage people to set appointments instead of relying so much on spontaneous drop-in visits. Just a simple one-on-one meeting once a day, or once a week, could work miracles in your schedule.

To help bunch their items together, some people keep a notebook, assigning one page per name and writing down the topics they wish to discuss on the pages. Periodically, they call or meet with each person to go over the accumulated items. One good technique is to write your question or comment on the left side of the page, then to use the right side of the page to note the replies you receive.

People variously prefer to collect items in file folders, boxes, trays, or even wall pocket files. One creative person used a white board and marker pens. He divided the board into several grids and assigned one name per grid. He made notes in the grids. When he called to discuss the items, he erased each as it was covered. When he had erased all the items, he said goodbye. If not a white board, you could use a bulletin board. Thumbtacks or pushpins could hold notes under different groupings.

However you do it, bunching items together is a great idea. Start with yourself, then try to convince others to do it too. If everyone bunched their routine interruptions, half our interruption problems would disappear overnight. Fortunately, the more we learn to work effectively in teams, the more we begin to appreciate the jobs our teammates perform. This appreciation should help us realize how important it is to keep interruptions to a minimum.

Taming the Telephone

Telephones are essential. Everyone knows that. But they can also be a waste of time. It depends on how you use them. For example, many people spend at least two or three hours on the telephone every day. Studies show, however, that about half of all "business" calls aren't about business. Even calls that start out dealing with relevant topics often deteriorate into trivia. Poorly conducted conversations don't accomplish much.

Plan your calls before you dial. Planning makes your calls more productive and shortens the time you spend on the phone. To plan your calls, ask yourself why you are calling. What result do you intend to achieve? After you clarify your purpose, consider how to accomplish it. What words should you use? What sequence or structure should you follow? How should you position your points, or phrase your questions?

Consider, too, how much time you are going to need. Most people are short on time. If you need more than a few minutes, you may want to arrange a telephone appointment. Telephone appointments aren't as common as face-to-face appointments, but for time-conscious people they make a lot of sense.

Give careful thought to your opening remarks. Realize that whenever you make an unexpected call, you are creating an interruption for the other person that may cause resentment. The mere fact that the phone rings is an irritation. Therefore, many people are not in a positive frame of mind as they answer the phone. At the very least, they weren't thinking about you or your problems. For goodness sake, don't waste their time chatting about the weather. Skip the small talk and get right to the point.

When someone answers, give that person complete information. "Hello. This is Merrill Douglass. I'm calling Fred Anderson about our pending contract. Will you please connect us?" This not only saves time on questions but will also get you connected more often.

Close your calls promptly. If the other party seems to be drifting, serve notice that you are ready to hang up. "Before we hang up, Chris, I'd like to review what I need to deliver to you" is a tactful way to indicate that you are just about finished with the conversation.

Consider alternatives. In 1990, AT&T reported that the chances are only one in six that you will reach the person you're calling on the first try. It might be better to send a fax, electronic note, postcard, or letter.

Keep records of incoming calls. Find out who calls, when, and about what. Analyze this record to determine who should answer your telephone. Generally speaking, the higher your level in the organizational hierarchy, the greater the probability is that answering your own phone is a timewaster.

Train people to answer your telephone effectively. Consider what they should say and how they should say it. Which questions should they ask? What information will you need either to act on the call or to delegate it to someone else? When and how should callers be referred to others?

Trimming Telephone Tag

Part of your phone time is spent playing telephone tag. Someone calls when you're out and so leaves a message. When you return the call, he's gone, so you leave a message. Then he calls again, you call again, and round and round it goes. Telephone tag is frustrating. According to one study, you could waste over two years of your life just playing telephone tag. Here are some tips to help you reduce the problem.

Ask people you call often when they are most likely to be in, and call at these times whenever you can. Tell them the best time to call you, too.

If the person you are calling is not available, ask if another person can help you. You may find that someone else can help you even faster and better than the person you were trying to reach.

Rather than leaving a message that you called, you may prefer to call again. If you reach a secretary, ask when the person you are trying to reach is most likely to return. Ask what time would be best to call. Maybe you can even set up an appointment for a telephone meeting.

If you must leave a message, be sure it's a complete message. The vast majority of messages left contain only a name and a number. Leaving a complete message increases your chances of a successful result. Tell the person you talk to or the answering machine who you are, why you are calling, where you can be reached, and when is the best time to call you. Be sure to mention anything else the other person will need in order to help you. With a complete message, the other person has more options for helping you even if he can't call you back personally. If nothing else, he can leave you the answer when he gets your machine on the callback.

If you have the choice between leaving a message with a person or on voice-mail, think very carefully. Many people prefer voice-mail because they have complete control over the message. If you leave a message with a person, you have no control. That person may or may not deliver the message as you gave it.

Finally, look for alternative ways to contact people. Many people find that fax machines, electronic mail, voice-mail, or cellular phones all help reduce the telephone tag problem. Many people conclude their business simply by leaving messages on each other's answering machines.

Curbing Socializing

Socializing is one of the biggest hazards of working in teams. Teams demand more face-to-face contact. Teammates may even share the same office space. Under these circumstances, it's easy for conversations to drift off work topics and onto other things. This is especially true when teammates are also friends off the job.

Socializing is like aspirin: A little helps a lot, but too much can be deadly. The most oppressive office we've ever seen had strict rules against employees talking to each other at any time. On the other hand, we've been in offices where people have trouble getting anything done because of all the social chatter. Of course we need to talk to each other. Communication is the grease that keeps the team working smoothly. The issue is one of degree.

We want to continue the necessary socializing and stop the unnecessary part. Just because we're teammates, working on the same project, doesn't automatically mean that every conversation is important. Learn to recognize what helps and what hinders. Remember, too, that while three or four of you are standing around talking you may also be creating a big problem for anyone else in the same vicinity who is trying to work.

Many of us now work in open office arrangements, where we have cubicles with partitions, but no doors. It's common to see people clustered in the walkways around some particular cubicle, noisily engaged in chit-chat. This can be a major distraction to anyone within hearing distance. It's not just that your socializing blocks your own productivity, it may also prevent others from getting something done.

Unnecessary socializing may stem from habit, ego, curiosity, the desire to be liked, or even procrastination. We've noticed that when people don't want to do a particular job, they are very likely to talk to someone else, either in person or on the phone. Learn to recognize your actions for what they are. You can reduce your socializing without becoming antisocial.

Unnecessary socializing can also result from casual contacts. The other person may not even be looking for you. In cases like this, it may help to rearrange your furniture so that you don't face the door. If people passing by can easily see your face, they are more likely to stop and visit.

Carefully consider the flow of work and people when organizing your office. Poor arrangements create problems. Items like coffee pots and copy machines inevitably attract people. Try putting them out of the way where they will do minimal damage. It's hard to get much work done when there is a minor convention meeting around the coffee pot next to your desk.

Reducing Distractions

Most offices are full of distractions—phones ringing, people talking, people coming and going, printers clattering, radio stations playing boring canned music in the background, construction noise, and who knows what else. How can you concentrate with all this happening? Here are a few suggestions on how to cope with distractions.

- *Reduce the noise levels on all utilities, office machines, or electronic devices.* For instance, lower the volume on the phones. You might consider shutting off the ring completely. Blinking lights often work as well as bells or buzzers. Use features like call-forwarding to kick in on the first ring.

Look for ways to reduce the volume on anything that produces a noise. Put covers on dot matrix printers or replace them with quieter laser printers. Put copiers in separate rooms and close the door. Remove all radios, stereos, or televisions. Replace the ballast in the fluorescent lights if they are buzzing loudly.

Use white noise in the background. White noise machines generate sounds at wavelengths that effectively mask many ordinary office noises. Most people won't even realize it exists, yet it will effectively cover many distracting sounds.

- *Put rugs or carpets on the floor, or ask people to wear soft-soled shoes.*

- *Put sound-absorbing materials on the walls.* Visit any up-to-date radio station or recording studio to see the variety of materials available.

- *Try wearing earphones, the bigger the better.* Even sucking on hard candy or lozenges or chewing gum can help you block out distractions.

- *Place coffee machines and water fountains as far away as possible from where people are working.* Segregate these inevitable social centers.

- *Train yourself to ignore nearby conversations.* Rearrange your office furniture if that will help prevent unwelcome visitors or distracting socializing. If necessary, find a place to hide when you desperately need quiet time.

- *Analyze your floor plan and arrange it so that people who must interact often are placed close together.* This not only saves time for the people involved, it also cuts down on the distractions and interruptions for others.

- *Get everyone together and ask them to brainstorm the distraction problem.* When people brainstorm a problem, they almost always come up with ingenious and workable solutions.

• *Finally, stop mentally procrastinating and get down to work.* If you are dragging your feet on some project, you're probably looking for something to interrupt you, and most anything will do. The more you get involved with your work, the less you'll notice many of the distractions around you.

As long as we work with others there are bound to be interruptions. While we can't control everything that happens during the day, we can control our response to what happens. Our responses, in turn, determine much of the impact the events of the day have on us.

Interruptions are part of working in teams. They're part of your job. But that doesn't mean you must be at the mercy of whatever interruptions occur. You can improve conditions. You can't control everything, but you can probably control more than you realize.

Interruptions are people. Remember to be gracious with people—but firm with time. You don't have to be rude. Practice prevention and reduction techniques whenever you can. Here's another case where the Golden Rule applies. Interrupt others with the same reluctance or consideration you would wish them to use when interrupting you.

11

Managing the

Boss

In Chapter 6, we said that ineffective communication was probably the greatest timewaster of all. If we were asked to name the runner-up for the title, we'd reluctantly have to say it was the boss. In Chapter 1, we pointed out that the day of "the boss" is dying, and we expect to see far fewer of them in the future. Unfortunately, we aren't there yet. There are still too many bosses out there, and they hinder more than they help. Poor bosses are not only a major deterrent to developing good teams, they are a major source of team timewasting as well.

This does not mean that all managers waste team time. Many don't. We've had the privilege of seeing many excellent managers who inspire their teams to almost unbelievable results. We wish that everyone could work with one of these people. Nor does it mean that all complaints are valid. Many aren't. But all too often wasted time can be traced directly to a boss.

For example, the boss is often the biggest interrupter in the office. A disorganized boss loses things, creates bottlenecks, and virtually ensures crises. A boss who fails to clarify objectives or to take time for good planning will be constantly switching priorities. Bosses who procrastinate create grief for everyone.

Some bosses are aware of the problem, but others aren't. Some even refuse to consider the possibility of such a problem. In the latter case, you're usually better off looking for a better boss. For now, though, let's consider a condition we've often encountered: The boss is not aware that he or she is creating time problems or doesn't know the extent of the problems created. Even good bosses, with the best of intentions, can fall into this trap.

Why is the boss unaware? One reason is that most of us lack the courage to speak up. Many of us feel intimidated by our bosses. It may even be the title, more than the individual, that's intimidating. Nevertheless, because we feel intimidated, good, and especially necessary, communication is thwarted.

Here's a common example: Your boss gives you an additional assignment, but doesn't specify the priority of the new task or its due date. You fail to ask for clarification and automatically drop something more important to work on the new assignment first. This, of course, often leads to a crisis on the job that has been put aside. You complain that the boss is a timewaster and the boss complains about incompetent help.

Who's at fault? That's easy; you both are, but the boss is still the boss, and you suffer most. How do you solve the problem? That's much harder. What's worse, many of us aren't even trying to solve the problem. It's easier to find scapegoats than solutions.

A good approach would be to consider three general principles of behavior. First, talk usually precedes action. You and your boss must discuss the problem together before a solution is likely. It takes dialogue. But what kind of dialogue is needed, and how can it be developed?

That's where the second principle comes in: A dialogue based on facts is the kind most likely to lead to agreement. Whatever is talked about and however it's done, the anticipated result should be agreement on how to solve the problem. Recall from our discussion of facts versus inferences in Chapter 6 that facts lead to agreement, whereas inferences lead to disagreement.

You must also decide on who owns the problem, because that's where the third principle applies: People seldom solve problems unless they first recognize them as problems. You may think there is a problem that needs solving, but does your boss agree? In fact, the boss-as-timewaster problem almost always requries joint action, which in turn depends on your both seeing the same problem.

The solution depends on developing a dialogue that focuses on the facts and leads to agreement about the problem. Commitment to solving the problem is then much easier. How do you do all this? Believe it or not, a time log is an excellent starting point.

Let's suppose that the boss is one of your biggest timewasters. Is your boss aware of this? Maybe, maybe not. Remember, we spend most of our time thinking about ourselves, and that includes your boss too. In other words, your boss probably spends very little time thinking about your job or your problems. If you suggest that your boss is creating a problem for you, he or she may honestly believe just the opposite. Conversations that are based only on subjective opinion produce few improvements.

Instead of engaging in a possibly futile discussion, keep a time log on where your time goes. What do you do, when do you do it, and why? If the boss is a problem, it will show up. If the boss does not appear as a time problem in your log, you should reassess your perceptions.

Let's assume, however, that the boss problem is reflected in your time log. Now you have objective data, not simply a subjective solution that could easily sound like complaining. Sharing this information will quickly make the boss aware of the problem. The ensuing dialogue then has a much higher probability of producing a workable solution.

To talk to your boss, you might begin like this: "I've been concerned about making the best use of my time on this job. I decided to record a time log and analyze exactly where my time is spent now. I'd like to share the results of that analysis with you." Very few bosses will refuse such an approach.

As you discuss the results of the time log, point out your strengths and weaknesses. Indicate to your boss the steps you have already taken to solve some of your time problems. In the midst of the discussion, say to the boss, "Here's another problem that I need you to help me solve." Then, describe how your boss is presenting a time problem for you.

At this point, you will discover that your boss is either already aware of the problem or that there is no awareness. The discussion will solve the unawareness issue. Once the boss is aware, he or she will be either concerned or unconcerned about improving the situation. If the boss is not concerned with improving, you have just discovered another fact about your job. You can accept the situation and go on from there, or you can look for a new boss.

If the boss is concerned, he or she has the option to act to improve the situation or not to act. Whether or not the boss acts depends in part on the extent to which you and the boss develop an action plan. Be sure to discuss how to implement your plan effectively.

What do you have to lose? The very worst that can happen is that your boss will question the manner in which you collected your data. The boss may believe that you made a mistake in recording activities. This is highly improbable, but let's assume that it happens. Your next step is to agree with the boss, and to suggest that you both keep a time record for a week or two. In this case, your position can only be strengthened in that the time problem is sure to show up in your boss's time log as well as in yours.

Assessing Yourself

Sometimes, the boss may not be guilty. The problem may instead lie with you. For example, a friend of ours was once denied a promotion he felt he deserved. Another manager was given the job and wound up as Bob's superior. Unfortunately, his new boss did not understand the job nearly as well as Bob did. As a result, he spent a great deal of time talking with Bob, relying on Bob, and interrupting Bob in order to gain a working knowledge of the department. Bob said his new boss was creating a major time problem for him. In fact, whatever Bob's new boss did, Bob interpreted it negatively.

After discussing this situation, we suggested that Bob stop

fighting and approach his new boss differently. On the assumption that the boss was not as qualified as Bob, we thought that Bob's best strategy would be to do all he could to make his new boss look good.

It took Bob several weeks before he could agree to this approach. However, once he did, he discovered many ways in which to help his boss. Within a few months, Bob had helped his boss look so good that the boss was promoted again and Bob himself was promoted to head the department—the position he had wanted in the first place.

We often get so engrossed in looking at a situation from our own particular point of view that we are reluctant to admit there could even be another point of view. Sometimes looking at things from another perspective helps us realize that we are responsible for a greater portion of the problem than we thought. Other people are not always the culprit.

Try assessing yourself from the boss's viewpoint. Here are several questions to get you started. Ask them as if you were the boss, evaluating you!

- Is this person's overall performance good?
- How cooperative is this person?
- How much has this person helped to improve the job?
- How well does this person try to communicate with me?
- How dependable is this person?
- Does this person ever embarrass me or talk about me behind my back?
- In what way does this person make a difference in our operation?
- Does this person bring me solutions as well as problems?
- What is the quality of this person's work?
- Does this person usually meet deadlines?
- Does this person get along well with other teammates?
- Is this person a team player?

Add any other questions to the list that seem appropriate to you. The whole idea is to try seeing yourself through your boss's eyes.

Communicating With the Boss

Open communication channels are essential for good relations with the boss. As long as you're talking together, all kinds of things are possible. It's when you stop talking that serious problems develop.

How can you tell whether or not communications are good between you and your boss? If you can answer yes to all the following items, you've got near perfect conditions. Every item you answer no to signals something that could be improved.

- Can you ask for help without being embarrassed?
- Does your boss recognize the good things you do?
- Do you clearly understand exactly what the boss expects from you?
- Does your boss provide coaching when you need help on some aspect of the job?
- Do you know the reasons behind the major decisions your boss made this year?
- Does your boss understand your personal goals?
- Do you know at least two specific things you could do to get a better rating at your next performance review?
- Does your boss tell you when you miss the mark without putting you down?
- Are you free to disagree with your boss?
- Is your boss aware of the basic problems you cope with in doing your job?
- Do you know what objectives your boss is trying to reach?
- Are you aware of the major pressures affecting your boss?
- Do you know in what way your boss prefers to receive information?
- Are you aware of what you do that upsets your boss?
- Do you believe it is your responsibility to find a way to work with your boss?

Perhaps an important point to realize is that improving the boss-as-timewaster problem will often require your initiative.

Most bosses aren't as aware of the problem as you are. Waiting for the boss to take the initiative only prolongs the problem— maybe indefinitely.

The belief that bosses are unapproachable is largely unfounded. Most bosses are human too. They share the same concerns. Many bosses intuitively know that they waste their subordinates' time and are anxious to help improve conditions. Good boss management will help both of you to use time more effectively.

Dealing With Problem Bosses

According to Drs. Mardy Grothe and Peter Wylie,* every boss in one way or another is a problem to his or her employees. Most bosses don't think of themselves as problem bosses, however. Part of the difficulty is that most bosses, whether they want to be or not, are insulated from feedback. Very few employees volunteer information to their bosses about the problems they cause. And because no one tells them what's wrong, they figure that they must be doing pretty well.

Another major reason for problem bosses, Grothe and Wylie claim, is that many bosses illustrate the Peter Principle when it comes to managing people. They have been promoted because they were good workers, not necessarily because they are good with people. However, to be an effective boss requires strong interpersonal skills.

Many bosses have a strong dose of the Time Taskmaster temperament in their makeup. Unless they work at building up the positive side of their temperament, they usually drift toward the weaknesses of that temperament. When this happens, they tend to ignore people, manipulate them, and humiliate them. They're insensitive to individual differences and unwilling or unable to adjust to those differences. They often create win-lose situations, where the boss always wins. They seldom praise good work or provide much positive recognition. They can be very abrasive.

*Mardy Grothe and Peter Wylie, *Problem Bosses* (New York: Facts on File Publications, 1988).

With problem bosses, you have several options. First of all, you can do nothing. This may be a good strategy when either you or your boss will be in the job for only a short time. You may also accept them the way they are and go on from there. You might want to try changing the boss, although this can be difficult. You may have more luck talking to him or her in a group rather than individually. You can also change yourself or your perceptions. Or, if the situation seems hopeless, you can always look for a new boss.

Probably the best strategy is to try managing your boss. This is usually a good idea whether or not you perceive the boss as a problem. Find out what the boss wants and needs, and try to provide it. There are many ways you can provide for your boss's needs without compromising yourself or your integrity. Adjust your work style to complement your boss's style. What is your boss's temperament? Use the insights gained from Chapters 3, 4, and 5 to improve your efforts to build a good relationship with your boss. Find out what your boss expects, and do your best to deliver it. Keep your boss informed. Be dependable and honest. And use your boss's time wisely.

Here are twelve other tips to help you manage your boss well:

1. *Discuss goals, plans, and priorities regularly.* The more both of you know what the other is up to, the easier it is to coordinate your activities and help each other.
2. *Offer solutions whenever you discuss a problem.* Don't expect your boss to have all the answers for solving your problems.
3. *Be sure to clarify responsibility and authority issues on new assignments.* Don't get trapped into accepting an assignment unless you have adequate authority to carry it out.
4. *Treat your boss as your best customer.* Compensate for his or her weaknesses. Zig where the boss zags. Catch him or her doing something good. Make it easy to work with you.

5. *Take pride in your work.* Do it to the best of your ability. Strive for excellence.
6. *Do your work promptly.* It's always better to finish something sooner than expected than to turn it in later than expected.
7. *Do everything you can to make your boss look good, especially to his or her boss.* When you fail, your boss fails too.
8. *Keep lines of communication open.* Be straightforward and honest. When you don't know, ask. If you think something can be improved, explain why. As long as the two of you keep talking, there is hope.
9. *Be patient and understanding.* You may never know what kinds of pressures and problems your boss may be coping with. His or her reactions may have nothing to do with you at all.
10. *Treat your boss as you'd want to be treated if you were the boss.* It's amazing how well this works—and how quickly you might become the boss.
11. *Learn how to match your personality style to your boss's style.* Look beyond the little irritating quirks and habits.
12. *Learn to see both the strengths and weaknesses of your boss.* Realize that the greater the strengths, the greater the weaknesses are likely to be. Accentuate the strengths.

Breaking In a New Boss

When a new boss arrives, does it make you a little nervous and apprehensive? Reorganizations, mergers, acquisitions, growth, and matrix teams all have at least one thing in common. They often bring a new boss onto the scene together with lots of uncertainty. Whenever a new boss comes in, everyone is suddenly on probation, although many people don't realize it. It's a new ball game, a new set of rules, brand-new expectations. Whether you survive or suffer depends on how astute you are.

Here are several guidelines for making a positive adjustment to a new boss.

- *Remember that what worked in the past may not work in the future.* Assuming that it will can be a deadly trap.
- *Do everything you can to create a good first impression.* The first impression is often a lasting impression.
- *Be flexible and open to change.* Don't dwell on the way things were done in the past. New conditions may call for new procedures.
- *Help your new boss as much as you can.* Remember that the boss has to adjust to a new situation too. In fact, the boss may need you as much as you need the boss.
- *Find out which objectives and priorities are most important to your new boss.*
- *As problems and questions come up, deal with them honestly and openly.* Don't go behind your boss's back, and don't complain to others about your boss.
- *Do everything you can to make your new boss look like a winner.* Help him or her achieve positive results.
- *Be prepared for change.* Some things are beyond your control. Too often we greet a new boss with resistance or even resentment. These reactions seldom help. Instead, accept the new boss as gracefully as you can, and approach him or her with a positive strategy. If you expect things to work out well, they probably will.

Yes, some bosses do cause time problems and a lot of others as well. But with a little patience and understanding—plus some initiative and lots of hard work—you can resolve many of them. We think that's much better than simply continuing to complain about the problem while doing nothing to fix it.

12

Teaming Up With

Secretaries

If current trends continue, we can expect to see fewer secretaries in the future. More of us will be sharing secretaries, and many of us will have no secretary at all. In cutting secretaries, some companies have gone too far. It is not unusual to find team members who spend 30 to 50 percent of their time doing routine work that secretaries used to do.

Lack of secretarial assistance cuts into the time available for other contributions. No doubt about it, a good secretary can double your worth to the organization. Yet, in spite of the potential, many secretaries are poorly trained, badly treated, and grossly underutilized.

At the very least, people fortunate enough to still have a secretary must think of themselves and their secretary as a team. Secretaries, in fact, are often among the most valuable players on a team and should be better recognized for the contribution they make. To do otherwise perpetuates the problems of the past. Changing to a team focus opens up new possibilities in the way you work together.

Your Current Relationship With Your Secretary

How well do you use your secretary? Are you and your secretary pulling in the same direction? Even if you are reasonably pleased with the results, perhaps you realize that they could still be improved. Here's a quiz that will get you thinking about your relationship with your secretary.

1. Do you always tackle things on the basis of priority?   Yes   No
2. Do you frequently switch signals or priorities on your secretary?   Yes   No
3. Do you take enough time to provide good instructions and keep communication flowing freely between you and your secretary?   Yes   No
4. Do you have confidence in your secretary's ability to handle routine activities and keep trivia away from you?   Yes   No
5. Do you delegate as much as you can to your secretary?   Yes   No
6. Do you use dictating machines instead of dictating personally to your secretary?   Yes   No
7. Do you always keep your secretary informed about what is happening?   Yes   No
8. Do you and your secretary review your daily plan, schedule, and priorities?   Yes   No
9. Is your secretary a good sounding board for ideas and problem solving?   Yes   No
10. Is your office well organized and free of clutter?   Yes   No
11. Do you frequently interrupt your secretary?   Yes   No
12. Do you always treat your secretary as an important and unique team member?   Yes   No
13. Do you always take the time to listen?   Yes   No
14. Do you compliment your secretary more than you criticize?   Yes   No
15. Do you regularly discuss the specific responsibilities of your secretary's job?   Yes   No
16. Do you take the initiative in resolving conflicts that arise between yourself and others who share your secretary's services?   Yes   No

17. Do you encourage your secretary to express   Yes   No
    initiative and resourcefulness?
18. Can you easily accept constructive criticism from   Yes   No
    your secretary?
19. Do you consistently encourage and support your   Yes   No
    secretary's efforts to improve and develop?
20. Do you complain about your secretary to co-   Yes   No
    workers or others?

If you truthfully answered yes to all the questions except
for questions 2, 11, and 20, you're in pretty good shape. You
probably have a healthy, thriving relationship with your secretary. Good for you! If you answered no to several of the
questions (or yes to questions 2, 11, and 20), read the following
pages carefully. Act to improve areas where you are negligent.

Transforming the Relationship

How do you begin to transform your present relationship with
your probably underused and unfulfilled secretary into something better? Tradition and habit are powerful forces in people's
lives. People often choose the status quo, no matter how
depressing, over efforts that could lead to positive change. The
first step toward the professional team relationship we advocate here is the biggest one. It involves taking a second look at
your secretary and realizing that perhaps your secretary, too,
wants something more. Not all secretaries, of course, want
or can handle additional responsibility. But most of them do,
and can.

Unfortunately, there are limited materials available for
teaching us how to use secretaries effectively. Where do we
learn? Most of us have learned by observing how other people
deal with their secretaries. If we have a positive role model, we
learn good things. If we emulate a poor model, the results are
negative.

The road to better results with your secretary begins with
self-study. The following questions will help you get started:

- How, specifically, has your secretary helped you most?
- How could your secretary best help you in your most important responsibilities?
- What are you doing that could be done by your secretary?
- What do you wish your secretary were doing that he or she is not now doing?
- What prevents you from delegating more to your secretary?
- What are your secretary's strongest points or skills?
- What specific steps can you take to upgrade your secretary's skills?
- What suggestions from your secretary do you resist most?
- What actions can you take immediately toward creating a better relationship with your secretary?

These questions will help you focus on the particular needs of both you and your secretary. Try to be as specific as possible in your responses.

A personal time log may also be helpful. It will routinely point to the rough spots in your day-to-day activities and provide direction for your improvement efforts. If your secretary also keeps a time log, your potential benefits are increased. With two logs, you can make a comparison for greater insight into the time problems you may be creating for each other.

You and your secretary must develop an ongoing dialogue about what wastes time and what uses time to the best advantage. Your time logs can help you do this. Another way to develop a dialogue is by completing the manager's timewaster profile and the secretary's timewaster profile shown in Figures 12-1 and 12-2.

Developing the manager's timewaster profile is easy. Just follow these five steps:

Step 1: In column 1, identify and rank your top six timewasters from the list shown in Figure 12-1. These are the timewasters most frequently identified by managers and professionals.

Figure 12-1.   The manager's timewaster profile.

Manager's Timewaster Profile

FREQUENTLY IDENTIFIED TIMEWASTERS	LISTING BY MANAGER		LISTING BY MANAGER'S SECRETARY		MANAGER'S COMBINED LISTING	
	Rank (1)	Weight (2)	Rank (3)	Weight (4)	Combined Weight (5)	Final Ranking (6)
Interruptions, distractions						
Involved in too much detail						
Crises, firefighting						
Unclear objectives or priorities, poor daily or weekly planning						
Meetings						
Paperwork						
Leaving tasks unfinished, jumping around from task to task						
Attempting too much at once, inability to say no						
Cluttered desk or office						
Ineffective communication, failure to listen						
Socializing, idle conversation						
Ineffective delegation, doing things myself						
Failure to do first things first						
Waiting for things, looking for things						
Procrastination, indecision, daydreaming						
Constantly switching priorities						
Organizational politics						
Unclear directions or instructions						
Poor follow-up						

Step 2: Weight your top six timewasters in column 2 as follows:

No. 1 timewaster = 30 points
No. 2 timewaster = 25 points
No. 3 timewaster = 20 points
No. 4 timewaster = 15 points

Figure 12-2. The secretary's timewaster profile.

Secretary's Timewaster Profile

FREQUENTLY IDENTIFIED TIMEWASTERS	LISTING BY SECRETARY		LISTING BY SECRETARY'S MANAGER		SECRETARY'S COMBINED LISTING	
	Rank (1)	Weight (2)	Rank (3)	Weight (4)	Combined Weight (5)	Final Ranking (6)
Unclear objectives, priorities, daily plans						
Attempting too much at once						
Inability to say "no"						
Poor office procedures, equipment problems, inadequate filing system						
Socializing, idle conversation						
Procrastination, indecision, daydreaming						
Cluttered desk or office						
Leaving tasks unfinished, jumping from task to task						
Interruptions, distractions						
Mistakes, poor training, ineffective performance						
Overcontrol by manager, lack of independence						
Switching priorities, confused priorities						
Unclear instructions, incomplete information						
Not being kept informed by manager						
Interruptions by manager, working for disorganized manager						
Errands, making copies, getting coffee, etc.						
Redoing work due to incorrect dictation, instructions from manager						
Ineffective communication, failure to listen						
Waiting for things, looking for things						

No. 5 timewaster = 10 points
No. 6 timewaster = 5 points

Step 3: Have your secretary identify and rank your top six timewasters in column 3. Your secretary should do this independently, without looking at your rankings. Weights should then be assigned to the secretary's rankings in column 4, using the weighting scheme as given.

Step 4: Add the weights in columns 2 and 4 for each timewaster identified. Record the combined weights in column 5.

Step 5: Record the final ranking for your timewasters in column 6. The timewaster with the greatest combined weight is No. 1, the timewaster with the second biggest combined weight is No. 2, and so on. In case of equal weightings, use the secretary's rank order as a guide.

The secretary's timewaster profile is developed in similar fashion. The timewasters on the secretary's profile are the ones most frequently identified by secretaries. In columns 1 and 2, your secretary identifies and ranks his or her top six timewasters. You identify, rank, and weight the secretary's top six timewasters in columns 3 and 4. Weights and scoring are the same as for the manager's profile.

This exercise provides an independent and joint assessment of both your timewasters and your secretary's timewasters. When the profiles are completed, analyze them carefully. Look for relationships between the manager's profile and the secretary's profile. Does each person seem to create problems for the other? Generally, improvement for one is very difficult unless the other also improves. This is especially true for your secretary. Unless you use your time well, it may be impossible for your secretary to do so.

Quite often, solutions as well as problems emerge from the profiles. Managers and secretaries commonly cause time problems for each other. This need not be. Identifying the problems makes it easier for each person to change. Working on them together helps both of you improve faster.

What Should a Secretary Do?

Exactly what should a good secretary do? The 42 duties listed in Figure 12-3 are based on a prototype job description from Professional Secretaries International. Go over this list with your secretary and discuss how to improve on any dimension that's lacking or poorly developed.

Figure 12-3. The duties of an executive secretary.

A professional secretary should:

1. Handle routine projects.
2. Handle administrative details.
3. Run errands.
4. Coordinate office procedures.
5. Maintain an efficient work flow.
6. Establish and maintain harmonious working relationships with others.
7. Schedule appointments.
8. Maintain calendars.
9. Screen/assist/refer visitors and callers.
10. Arrange business itineraries.
11. Arrange/coordinate travel requirements.
12. Use initiative and judgment to minimize the effect of the manager's absence.
13. Refer matters to delegated authority when the manager is gone.
14. Take manual shorthand.
15. Transcribe from machine dictation.
16. Type material from longhand or rough copy.
17. Keyboard copy into computer.
18. Sort/read mail and documents.
19. Annotate mail and documents.
20. Attach files/materials needed for action.
21. Determine routing for documents.
22. Determine signatures required.
23. Maintain follow-up.
24. Compose communications for the manager.
25. Sign the manager's name.
26. Research and abstract information.
27. Correlate/edit/organize materials from others.
28. Maintain filing systems.
29. Make copies.
30. Maintain records.
31. Maintain an up-to-date procedures manual.
32. Arrange meetings and conferences.
33. Record minutes of meetings.
34. Transcribe/distribute meeting minutes.

(continues)

Figure 12-3. Continued.

A professional secretary may also:

35. Supervise other employees.
36. Hire other employees.
37. Select/purchase supplies.
38. Select/purchase equipment.
39. Maintain budget.
40. Maintain expense account records.
41. Maintain financial records.
42. Maintain confidential files.

Some people argue that only a private secretary could do all these tasks. However, even secretaries serving two or three people can perform most of these duties. As the number of people served by one secretary expands, the list of possibilities decreases rapidly. The more people who are served by one secretary, the less that can be done for any one of them. But when secretaries are trained well and expected to do all the things on this list, their value to the team is very substantial.

The Shared Secretary

Not everyone has a private secretary. In many cases, private secretaries are simply not justified by the amount of work involved. Justified or not, the shared secretary is the trend of the future. This trend, however, leads to further complications in the secretary's role.

How many people should be served by one secretary? If you must spend your time doing what a secretary could do, you don't have that time for doing other things. Whether or not to add more secretaries should depend on the value of the alternative time use. Unfortunately, decisions regarding the degree of secretarial help to be made available are often based solely on the issue of direct cost, without consideration of indirect effects or opportunity costs.

On the other hand, not everyone who claims to need a

secretary really does. Use time logs to reduce differences of opinion as to the objective facts. Better work habits, the streamlining of paperwork, and the use of new technology may reduce the secretarial needs of many people. Our main point is that these things rarely reduce the need to zero. Arbitrary decisions usually err. It's better to study and analyze the issues.

When people share a secretary, conflict is inevitable. The people sharing the secretary often expect the secretary to resolve conflicts over whose work is to be done first. This is unfair and unrealistic. It is not the secretary's job to resolve such conflicts. This must be done by those sharing the secretary. Many hesitate to tackle the issue, and thus prolong and compound the problem. Delaying may even cause them to lose a good secretary.

There are several general approaches to resolving the conflict problem. If all the people involved are of equal status, you might try a first come, first served system. Or, you might assign priorities on the basis of the types of work involved. The people sharing the secretary must sit down together and work out a system that seems both equitable and efficient.

With people of unequal rank, there are other considerations. The top person may want to set secretarial priorities as though everyone were equal. This means that the boss stands in line just like everyone else.

More traditional managers, however, may insist that their work always come first. Although this may be their right, exercising it often works against the total team effort. For this reason, we usually don't recommend it.

No matter what system you decide to use for sharing your secretary's time, make sure that everyone abides by it. The more exceptions you allow, the weaker the system becomes. Before long, you won't have any system at all.

The main concern is to have the secretary spend his or her time in a way that is beneficial to everyone. The secretary should not be constantly pressured or besieged by last-minute rush jobs. With proper time management, last-minute emergencies can be minimized.

One possible solution to the shared secretary problem is

hiring part-time private secretaries. In many cases, this would be an improvement over current conditions. At the very least, an additional part-time secretary would eliminate some of the status problems that complicate sharing secretaries.

Guidelines for Effective Teamwork

Here are twenty-five guidelines for building a better relationship with your secretary. The more you practice them, the better they work.

1. Consider your secretary as an important member of your team. Be sure to include him or her in team meetings.
2. Treat your secretary with dignity and respect. Provide support and backup. Don't downgrade your secretary to a gofer.
3. Discuss goals, priorities, and plans with your secretary on a daily basis. Do it first thing every morning.
4. Don't constantly interrupt your secretary during the day. Bunch things together to keep interruptions at a minimum.
5. Coordinate activities with your secretary so that both of you can get as much done as possible.
6. Provide as much lead time as you can. Avoid last-minute rush jobs. Start earlier.
7. Discuss problems and ideas with your secretary. Ask for his or her ideas, suggestions, and opinions.
8. Provide the best office equipment.
9. Allow your secretary to organize you and your office procedures.
10. Tell your secretary where you are going, how you can be reached, and when you will return.
11. Keep your secretary fully informed about what is happening. Ask what he or she would like to know about your business, projects, goals, and priorities.
12. Expect the best. Provide for your secretary's profes-

sional development. Include your secretary in training and development programs.

13. Encourage other people to deal directly with your secretary on routine matters.
14. Don't expect a shared secretary to resolve the problems of working for multiple bosses. That's your responsibility.
15. Ask your secretary how you could manage your time better. Ask what your secretary might do that you are now doing.
16. Ask what you're doing that wastes your secretary's time or hinders her or his performance. Improve conditions.
17. Take time to provide clear instructions and complete information to your secretary the first time. Use good feedback techniques.
18. Be patient. Take time to listen to your secretary.
19. Allow for individual initiative. Don't expect your secretary to do things the way you do them. Don't compare her or him to your previous secretary either.
20. Protect your secretary's time. Help him or her find quiet time when needed.
21. Ask your secretary what he or she would like to know about your business, projects, objectives, priorities.
22. Encourage and support your secretary. Boost his or her self-esteem.
23. Don't complain about your secretary to other people. Never blame your secretary for your failures.
24. Express appreciation.
25. Practice the Golden Rule.

It is more important than ever that you use your secretary's time well. The two of you ought to become an excellent team. Think of you and your secretary as a single job unit rather than as two separate jobs. The only rationale for having a secretary is to enable you to accomplish more. Thinking of the two of you as a team helps you to focus on how both professionals can use their time most effectively, whether alone or together, to achieve a common purpose.

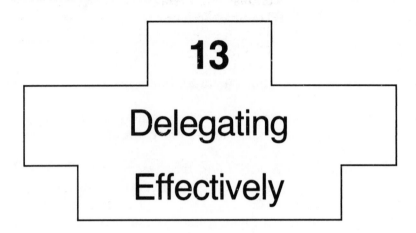

13

Delegating

Effectively

Delegation is a powerful concept for getting better results with teams. At the same time, it can be frustrating and difficult. On the one hand, it's a matter of how we feel about it; on the other, it depends how we approach it. Some people simply haven't learned how to do it right. We know we should delegate more, but we don't. We remember everything that went wrong when we delegated before. We decide to delegate less in the future so we won't get burned again.

There are two primary reasons for delegating: (1) because there is too much work for one person to handle, and (2) because it is an excellent tool for empowering and developing people on the team. So, whether you need help, or want more competent people around you, delegation is critically important.

Delegating today is different from what it once was. Historically, delegation was a vertical process, flowing downward through the chain of command from one superior to one subordinate. Vertical delegation followed the flow of formal authority through the organization.

Today, with a growing emphasis on self-directed work teams, horizontal delegation is as important as vertical delegation. Horizontal delegation involves delegating to peers or others over whom you have no formal authority. Some people, however, believe that when they have no formal authority they cannot delegate effectively. This isn't true.

The assumption from the past was that formal authority gave you the right to dictate to people: Do it, or else. But this was only partially true. Coercion did indeed bring about performance, but it could not ensure excellent, high-quality performance.

Mary Parker Follett six decades ago offered an alternative explanation that is more helpful.* She said you never have any more authority over another person than that person is willing to grant you. Your authority, in other words, depends on acceptance by the other person. This means that the only condition for delegating is that there be someone willing to accept what you want to delegate. Acceptance authority relies not on formal authority relationships but rather on your ability to persuade someone to do something.

This is a critical issue in today's organizations, especially for teams. Delegation involves peers as well as subordinates. The chain of command may have little or no real meaning in terms of everyday performance. Traditional autocratic management is no longer appropriate.

Reorganization, restructuring, and downsizing are potent forces changing the nature of organizations—and delegation. Matrix organizations mean multiple bosses. Self-directed work teams share the leadership roles in a variety of ways. Flatter organizations mean fewer managers with much wider spans of control. Managers are expected to be work team members as well as work team leaders.

The concept of work teams can be especially confusing. Some have no formal leaders at all. Some have revolving leaders. You may be the team leader on one project but only a team member on the next one. Yet you may find yourself working with the exact same people on both projects. Formal authority concepts are meaningless. No one may have

---

*Mary Parker Follett, "Some Discrepancies in Leadership Theory and Practice," in *Business Leadership*, ed. Henry Metcalf (London: Pitman, 1930).

the authority to hire, fire, reward, or penalize anyone else on the team.

Other complicating factors are the increasing number of knowledge workers and the push for more empowered employees. Subordinates increasingly have more technical competence than their managers have. They demand different treatment from their managers too. They expect to be more involved in the decision-making processes.

As organizations continue to evolve, delegation is more important than ever. It is the essence of empowering employees. Yet we need to move beyond the limitations of the old superior/subordinate model. Some definitions may be in order:

- *Delegation today means work sharing, whether it is vertical or horizontal.* It combines both formal position authority and acceptance authority. It means sharing responsibility and authority with others, and holding them accountable for performance.
- *Responsibility refers to the job assignment—the intended results.* It also includes the obligation to perform any activities necessary to achieve those results.
- *Authority refers to the right to act and make decisions.* Successful delegation requires authority equal to the responsibility.
- *Accountability means being called upon to answer for actions and decisions.* It also implies rewards and penalties.

For most of us, delegation involves a dilemma: We must keep what we want to give up—the responsibility; and we must give up what we want to keep—the authority. How well we handle this dilemma determines our success in delegating.

Fear of Delegating

We've all had both successes and failures with delegation. Theoretically, our successes should make us more confident about delegating in the future. It seems, though, that our failures have more impact on how we approach delegation, particularly when we are dealing with someone we have had no prior experience with.

We surveyed 135 managers about their delegation experiences. We asked about both vertical and horizontal delegation. What bothered them most about delegating? What were they afraid of? What did they worry about most? Here are some of their replies:

Vertical Delegation

"I might overload people."

"They won't do it, do it right, or do it on time."

"I can do it faster or better myself."

"I could do it in less time than it takes to explain to someone else."

"They won't do it my way, or I won't get what I wanted."

"They won't like it, they may resent it, or they may not accept it."

"They won't understand the job, or know how to do the job."

"They won't do it as well as I would."

"They may do it better than I could."

"They may see it as less important than I do."

"They won't feel the same sense of urgency I do."

"They won't report, won't report on time, or report in enough detail."

Horizontal Delegation

"They won't do it, or will give it back to me."

"They won't know what to do."

"They may wonder what I'm going to do, or may think this is part of my job."

"Their other jobs will take priority."

"They won't take it seriously, or they won't think it is very important."

"They will exceed their authority."

"They will leak confidential information."

"They will not have the same sense of urgency I have."

"They won't follow up, communicate, or coordinate things well."

"They will start out great, then drop the ball, and I'll wind up having to do it anyway."

"They won't work well with the group."

Vertical Delegation	*Horizontal Delegation*
"They won't plan, prepare, or coordinate things well."	"They're apathetic and I don't know how to motivate them."
"They will alienate others while doing the job."	"They will tell me everything is under control when it really isn't."
"They will make mistakes, and I'll have to do it over anyway."	"They won't do it right or do it on time."
"It's hard to delegate when I don't understand the goal myself."	"I feel guilty and don't want to overload them."
"I may be criticized by my superiors."	"I don't see them very often, it's hard to check on them, and I'll lose control of the job."
"My superiors may interfere with the job."	"It's hard to critique them and I have no recourse."
"I enjoy the job and don't want to give it up."	"I have to stroke their egos."

Many of these fears stem from low self-confidence. Some reflect a poor understanding of good delegation techniques. Still others flow from more traditional assumptions about authority relationships. Some can be traced to poor understanding of the new roles and relationships in work teams. Some are closely related to the personality characteristics discussed in Chapters 3, 4, and 5.

Our fears, warranted or not, hamper our attempts to delegate. Our fears could even become self-fulfilling prophecies. We act as if our fears are justified, and indeed, things work out that way. We must find ways to alleviate our fears, move ahead boldly, and act confidently. Otherwise, we wind up doing the wrong work, and everyone suffers.

Professor Peter Sassone of the Georgia Institute of Technology studied the impact of doing the wrong work. The results of his study are shown in Figure 13-1. As an employee's organizational level increases, the amount of lower-level work he or she does also increases. For example, managers spent 27 percent of their time doing their own level work, but 59 percent

Figure 13-1. Who does whose work?

Job Level	Time Spent Doing Own Level Work	Time Spent Doing Work Above Own Level	Time Spent Doing Work Below Own Level	Time Spent Doing Non-Productive Work
Managers	27%	1%	59%	13%
Senior Professionals	42	3	42	12
Junior Professionals	55	9	22	14
Technical Support	68	6	11	15
Administrative Support	85	5	0	10

Source: Data based on interviews with, and time logs kept by, 1,563 people in 77 offices, from a 1990–1991 study conducted by Peter Sassone of Georgia Institute of Technology.

of the time doing work that should have been done at lower levels.

You may want to analyze your own work load. How much of the work that you now do belongs at your organizational level? How much of what you're doing belongs on one or more levels below you? Pushing that work down the hierarchy produces three benefits: (1) It frees up some of your time for more vital activities; (2) it empowers people down the line as they are given more authority to act on a wider range of responsibilities; and (3) it saves money by transferring more of your work to less highly paid employees.

Delegating work to someone else, however, is seldom easy. The issue is trust, or the lack of it. It means that a portion of our rewards and penalties henceforth depends on someone else's performance. As fear increases, trust diminishes. When we're afraid, we tend to hold onto things, to defend our position, to control more tightly.

At times, we think we do trust the other person. Then, when called upon to delegate to her, we find we don't trust her as much as we thought we did. Sometimes we delegate a job, then turn around and take it back. Other times, we hover so constantly that we interfere significantly with the other person's ability to do the job. No matter what the symptom, it is fear that makes delegation so difficult.

> Delegation involves a dilemma: We must keep what we want to give up—the responsibility; and we must give up what we want to keep—the authority.

Learning to Delegate

You have to acknowledge your fears and confront them head-on before you can work out a way to deal with them. Denying them is useless. Examine them to see which ones are rational and which ones aren't. Talk them over with someone else.

To delegate effectively, you must recognize and accept the fact that some risk is inevitable. You must also learn to trust people in spite of that risk. When the risk is low, it's obviously easier to trust. And as trust grows, you can tolerate greater levels of risk.

Part of the risk in delegating depends on the approach. Improve the process and you lower the risk that something will go wrong. There is no magic involved, just a few guidelines to follow:

1. Think and plan first.
2. Clarify the job responsibilities.
3. Select the right person.
4. Decide on authority levels.
5. Set appropriate controls.
6. Maintain a motivating environment.
7. Hold the person you choose accountable.

If you have not delegated much in the past, you will probably experience greater anxiety as you begin to delegate more. You may worry a lot. You may tend to overcontrol people. You may spend more time than necessary checking up on what's happening. This will not save time. It may, in fact, require much more time than if you had done the job yourself. The solution is not to do the job yourself but to learn how to cope with your increased anxiety.

Guideline 1: Think and Plan First

One big reason we fail at delegating is because we don't think things through ahead of time. We're in a hurry and believe we can't take the time to think and plan properly. Not surprisingly, hasty delegation often turns out poorly. Why is it that we never have time to do it right the first time, but we always have time to do it over?

Here are several questions to help you think first before you delegate. They take very little time to answer, and they'll help improve your success rate.

1. Exactly what am I delegating? What results do I expect?
2. Who should do this particular job? Why this person rather than another?
3. How much do I trust this person?
4. How much authority will this person need to do the job well?
5. How will I control his or her performance? How much supervision will he or she need?
6. What checkpoints should I set up? When and how often should I check?
7. What guidelines, direction, or information will he or she need?
8. What motivates this person?

You may find it valuable to write out your responses. This forces you to spell out your answer to each question and prevents skipping over any of them glibly. You want to make sure that everything is well organized and clarified in your mind before you pass on the assignment to someone else.

Another good idea is to write out all the pertinent details

for the person you select. Use something like the delegation planner shown in Figure 13-2. People often forget verbal directions, or they misunderstand them, or they recall them differently at a later time. Putting it in writing obviates these potential problems. Notice that the delegation planner centers around the three primary issues: responsibility, authority, and accountability.

Fill out each section of the delegation planner before you speak to the person you have chosen. Use it as a guide for

Figure 13-2. A sample delegation planner.

Delegation Planner

Person	Project	Importance: H M L
		Urgency: H M L

RESPONSIBILITY: *Results To Be Achieved*	AUTHORITY LEVEL INTENDED
	1 = Get facts, I decide
	2 = Report pros and cons, I decide
	3 = Recommend action, I decide
	4 = Decide action, wait for my approval
	5 = Decide action, act unless I veto
	6 = Act, tell me what happens
	7 = Act, tell me if it is unsuccessful
	8 = Act, no report needed

ACCOUNTABILITY: *Controls, Checkpoints, Due Dates*

FOLLOW-UP: *Comments, Evaluations*

discussing the assignment. Be sure to explain each part. Modify it, if necessary, during your discussion. When you're finished, give the other person a copy to provide written confirmation of your agreement. It's like a contract between the two of you.

Remember, successful delegation starts before you actually delegate anything. If you think first, you'll automatically delegate better. You'll find it easier to cover all the bases, because you'll know what they are. You're also more likely to provide clear instructions and complete information from the outset. Think things through before you act, and the results are bound to be much better.

Guideline 2: Clarify the Job Responsibilities

Good delegation focuses on well-defined goals. Exactly what do you expect the other person to accomplish? If the job is done well, what do you expect to see? Spell this out clearly.

People sometimes fail to distinguish between delegating and simply assigning work. Delegating charges the other person with achieving a specific result. How to achieve the result is not specified. Assigning work usually focuses on getting someone to do specific activities, but does not necessarily involve specifying the end result of those activities. If you tell someone what to do and how to do it, you're probably assigning work and not delegating. Under delegation, the delegatee decides what to do and how to do it to achieve the desired result. Under assignment, the worker has very little leeway.

It's also a good idea to tell the other person how important and how urgent you consider the assignment. This enables him to fit it into everything else on his schedule. Otherwise, you run the risk of having what you intended misinterpreted.

Guideline 3: Select the Right Person

Understandably, most of us delegate more often to the people we trust most. This leads to a few overdeveloped people and many underdeveloped ones. For the best results, we ought to spread jobs out to a much greater extent.

Unfortunately, the right person for a particular assignment may not be the one you trust most. One of the prime reasons for delegating is to develop people. For some assignments, you should pick the best qualified person. For other assignments, though, you may be more concerned with training opportunities.

This does not mean that we should arbitrarily give someone a job if we know that person can't handle it. It simply means that most of us consistently underestimate people's capabilities. We need to take a bit more risk. One executive suggests that the best way to develop trust is to be away a lot. When you're gone much of the time, you are forced to delegate jobs to more people. The surprising thing, he said, is how well people usually perform.

Delegation helps broaden experience, develops judgment, and provides cross-training in a variety of tasks. Instead of asking who can do this best, ask: Who most needs this opportunity? Who needs what kind of training? How much coaching must be done? What training will be necessary?

The trouble with training and coaching is that they take more time. We often excuse our neglect because we don't have enough time. At best, though, this is a short-term strategy, and sooner or later it brings big problems. Long-term success demands that everyone be as well trained as possible.

Try to maintain an equitable balance among the jobs you delegate. If not, you're likely to overload some people and underutilize others. Either way, people may grow to resent your actions.

When you're choosing the right person for the job, keep that person's personality in mind. You will want to match your approach to that particular personality. Reviewing the discussion of personality styles in Chapters 3, 4, and 5 will help you develop a good strategy.

Time Taskmasters tend to share little authority because authority equals control. They tend to supervise closely and to step in to solve problems. When delegated to, they usually solve their own problems without going to a supervisor. They may also assume more authority than was intended by the delegator.

Time Teasers tend to be more democratic delegators and share greater amounts of authority more easily. They rely on verbal reporting and tend to forget to follow up on a timely basis. When delegated to, they take on new jobs eagerly but tend to fizzle out and miss deadlines.

Time Tarriers are willing to share lots of authority, but only if they really trust the other person. They tend to want more feedback, but do not require formal reporting. When delegated to, they need lots of affirmation, especially at the beginning of the task.

Time Tenders usually prescribe how the job should be done as well as the result to be achieved. They require more detailed, formal reports and often overcontrol in an effort to avoid mistakes. When delegated to, they seek lots of details about the job and return often with questions to make sure they do the job right.

Guideline 4: Decide on Authority Levels

Delegating requires sharing authority with another person. Yet authority is what we hate to relinquish. A common consequence is giving someone a job to do, but not giving that person enough authority to get it done. This is like asking someone to bake a cake, but then not allowing the baker to go into the kitchen.

Authority should match responsibility. Responsibility without authority creates frustration, resentment, and bottlenecks. You get lots of problems and few benefits.

To delegate successfully, we must trust the people we choose to some degree. The greater the trust, the more we can delegate to them. This is why we usually start by testing people with small jobs before we give them bigger ones. As they successfully perform each job, our trust grows.

Most people do not trust immediately, or even quickly. Because trust often develops slowly, delegation involves several options, or levels. Higher-level options require greater competence and greater trust. If your trust level is low, start with lower levels of authority.

There are eight generally acceptable levels of authority, which can be described in this way:

1. Get the facts; I'll decide what to do with them.
2. Decide on alternatives and tell me the pros and cons of each one; then I'll decide what to do.
3. Recommend a particular action, but I'll make the final decision.
4. Decide what to do, but don't act until you get my approval.
5. Decide what to do, and take action unless I say not to.
6. Take any necessary action, and tell me what happens.
7. Take any necessary action, but tell me the outcome only if it is unsuccessful.
8. Take care of it; no reporting is necessary.

The degree of authority you grant to people depends on many factors, including the complexity or importance of the task, the time constraints surrounding it, their expertise, and your confidence in them. Each level of authority has a purpose. The first four levels are mostly training levels. As people develop, you move from lower to higher levels. You should not delegate the same level of authority to an untrained person as you would to someone who is highly competent.

Unfortunately, many people fall into patterns when delegating. They tend to delegate to the same people all the time. Or they never delegate above the fourth level to anyone. Taking the time to examine your own delegation patterns may be time well spent. It will show where you ought to be improving.

Each level of authority also requires a different time investment on your part. For instance, more contact is required at lower levels. Some poeple are surprised to find that increased delegation brings them very little additional time. In general, to recover large amounts of time, you have to delegate above the fifth level.

Guideline 5: Set Appropriate Controls

The key to effective control is balance: not too much and not too little. If there's too little, we do lose control of what's going on. But too much control dampens creativity, demotivates the delegatee, and interferes with good performance. Unfortunately, most of us err on the side of too much control. We think more about how the controls will help us than about how they hinder the person to whom we have delegated the task. It would probably help if we could see control from their side as well as our own side.

Dr. Larry Baker describes a model that can help you in deciding how much control to impose. His risk-change matrix is shown in Figure 13-3. The amount of information required and the frequency of reporting desired vary with the degree of risk and the rate of change. With high risk and a high rate of change, we want lots of information reported frequently. When the risk and rate of change are low, we need less information and we need it less often.

High risk conditions call for more detailed reporting. Rapidly changing conditions call for more frequent reporting. Decide which cell your delegated tasks fall in, and this model can help you decide how much control to apply.

The 80-20 rule is another useful guide to establishing

Figure 13-3. The risk-change matrix.

	DEGREE OF RISK	
	High	**Low**
Fast	More information More often	Less information More often
RATE OF CHANGE		
Slow	More information Less often	Less information Less often

Source: Larry D. Baker, *Effective Delegation Workbook* (St. Louis, Mo.: Time Management Center, 1991).

controls. Only a few items are critical, while most things are trivial. Place your control checkpoints on the critical parts, or at the critical milestones.

Applying the management-by-exception principle could be a time-saving approach to control. As long as everything is going as expected, stay out of it. This leaves control of the work in the hands of the other person, who is thereby helped to further develop judgment and skills. When exceptions do occur, use them as learning opportunities. Don't jump in and fix the problem yourself. Instead, coach delegates into finding the right solution. Help them become good problem solvers. Step in yourself only as a last resort.

When delegatees need assistance, make them feel comfortable in talking about their problems with you. Listen to them. Show respect for their thoughts and opinions.

When checkpoints have been set up, be sure to honor them. Insist on timely reports. Forgetting or skipping over established checkpoints sends the wrong message.

Guideline 6: Maintain a Motivating Environment

Delegation functions best when the corporate culture emphasizes personal growth, development, innovation, creativity, human dignity, and mutual respect. If your organization does not stress these values, delegation will be less effective.

When you're delegating the job, express confidence in the other person's ability. Be positive. Built up your delegatee.

After you've delegated the job, get out of the way. Don't hover over people, watching their every move. Don't interfere, overrule, or reverse their decisions.

Allow for differences. Don't expect others to do everything the way you would have done it. There are usually several ways to reach the same result. Different doesn't mean wrong.

Allow for learning errors. Be careful not to insist on perfection. As Peter Drucker points out, "Managers are paid to get results, not to be perfect." In fact, most of us learn more from our mistakes than we do from our successes. If you never allow someone to make a mistake, you decrease that person's opportunity to grow and develop.

Match your management style to the situation. The matrix in Figure 13-4 shows the relationship between style and structure. Structuring refers to how closely you intend to control the job, or how much of the assignment is prescribed by you. Style refers to whether you are directive or participative in your interactions with the other person.

Directive managers do a lot of "telling," while participative managers do lots of "selling," usually by asking questions. Directive managers make the decisions, while participative managers let others take part in the decision process.

Style and structure decisions depend on the specific person and situation involved. As people grow and situations change, the degree of each varies. Effective managers switch back and forth to match these varying needs.

Guideline 7: Hold the Person You Choose Accountable

Accountability means having to answer to someone for your actions. Traditionally, you were accountable to your superiors. Today, you may also be accountable to your peers or work teams. The worst thing that can happen is for no one to hold you accountable. When there is no accountability, there are major problems.

Some assume that when you can't fire people, you can't

Figure 13-4. The style and structure matrix.

| | STYLE | |
	Directive	Participative
Low STRUCTURE	Tells little	Asks little
High	Tells lots	Asks lots

hold them accountable. Not true. Accountability simply implies the extension of rewards or penalties based on performance. And in this sense, social rewards may be as powerful as tangible or monetary ones.

Use praise, recognition, and appreciation to reward people when they do well. Tell them when they don't measure up and why. Do it tactfully and firmly. Don't glibly excuse poor performance.

Expectations play a key role here. People tend to perform according to the expectations others have of them. The more you expect—realistically—the more you get. Start out by sincerely expecting people to perform well. Convey that expectation to them as positively as you can, both in actions and in words. This establishes a powerful psychological contract at the very beginning.

Receiving Assignments

Not only do you delegate; you are also delegated to. You've probably been receiving assignments far longer than you've been giving them. In fact, how you delegate to others depends largely on how you have been delegated to in the past. Whether good or bad, your delegation style is an expression or reaction to your experiences as a delegatee.

All too often, the person receiving the assignment walks away with three things: (1) a new assignment; (2) an uncomfortable feeling; and (3) lots of unanswered questions: "What do they really expect me to do? How well am I expected to do it? When should it be done? How should it be done? How much authority do I really have? Where will I get the necessary resources? How should I start? How will I fit this new job in with everything else? What are my priorities?"

We've asked hundreds of people to tell us what bothers them most about being delegated to. Here are some of the most common responses:

- "They have no consideration for the other jobs I already have."

- "They don't understand what they're trying to delegate."
- "I'm suspicious about their hidden agendas."
- "Who will actually be responsible for the results?"
- "There is too much pressure to do it immediately."
- "There is too little lead time."
- "They give me too many instructions."
- "They don't give me enough direction."
- "They don't give me all the details or information I need."
- "It's difficult to coordinate assignments from multiple bosses."
- "No one helps me resolve the conflicting priorities."
- "They don't help me understand the assignment."
- "I can't remember all the details."
- "They don't put anything in writing."
- "They overload me."
- "They have a different sense of urgency."
- "They give me too little authority for the responsibility I'm saddled with."
- "They change goals or deadlines in midstream."
- "They overcontrol the job."
- "I feel dumped on."
- "If I do well, they reward me with more work."
- "They provide no feedback."
- "They give me no credit or recognition."
- "They never praise me for what I do."
- "I'm afraid to ask questions."
- "They saddle me with unrealistic expectations or deadlines."
- "They provide no direction at all."
- "They don't know the goal or the expected result."
- "They're ambiguous about budgets or resources available."
- "I can't get clarification when I need it."
- "They only give me trivial work, never anything important."
- "The job's already screwed up when I get it."
- "They won't give me ownership."

- "They take credit for my work."
- "They step in at the end and take all the glory."
- "They give it to me one day, and take it back the next."
- "They're always switching priorities."

Ideally, delegators would always do it right. There would be few initial problems, ambiguities, or unanswered questions. In a less than ideal world, however, delegatees must sometimes take the initiative.

The best way to avoid potential problems is to ask questions. Ask any questions necessary to clarify responsibility, authority, and accountability issues. If the delegator isn't using a delegation planner, you as the delegatee should. Fill it out while discussing the assignment, then give a copy to the delegator.

Delegation works best when it is a two-way, interactive process. We can't expect others to commit themselves whole-heartedly to something they don't fully understand. They should normally not be pushed into jobs for which they don't have the requisite skills or authority to ensure success.

Avoiding Reverse Delegation

Delegation rightfully flows from delegator to delegatee, whether vertically or horizontally. When it reverts to the delegator, trouble isn't far behind. Yet reverse delegation is a common occurrence in most organizations. It often takes place without the delegator even realizing what has happened.

It begins innocently enough, but the result is always the same. The delegator winds up making decisions and doing the work that the delegatee should be doing. In addition, the delegator faces increased time pressures from taking on part of the delegatee's job.

Bill Oncken used to humorously describe reverse delegation in his seminars, and later wrote a classic article on the subject.* It can happen like this. You're walking down the

*William Oncken, Jr., and Donald L. Wass, "Management Time: Who's Got the Monkey?" *Harvard Business Review*, November–December 1974.

hallway one day when you pass one of your people who greets you with, "Hi, boss. By the way, we have a problem with XYZ."

How can you turn your back on a problem? Isn't it part of a manager's job to solve problems? Yes and no. It's the "we" you must look out for. "We" may mean that the other person has a problem that he or she wants to shift to you.

Your job, as manager, is not just to solve problems. You must also train others to be good problem solvers. In his article, Oncken advises managers not to take over other people's monkeys. If you do, he warns, you will soon have more monkeys on your back than you can take care of. Furthermore, you won't have enough time to do your own job.

However, being a concerned manager and wanting to help, you listen. As your delegatee explains the problem, you find yourself in an impossible dilemma: You know just enough to get involved, but not enough to solve the problem on the spot. You probably say something like this: "You're right, that's quite a problem. I'll have to check into it and get back to you." This means the ball is now in your court. The monkey is now on your back. The next step is up to you.

A few days later, your delegatee stops by to see how you are doing. "Boss, about that problem we discussed the other day. How are you coming?" This is good follow-up, part of the supervising process. However, you are now the person who is being supervised!

Your challenge at all times is to make sure that the people who work on a problem are the ones who should be working on it. When others bring you a problem, your task is to help them solve it. You do this not by solving the problem for them but by helping them to solve the problem themselves.

If you are the victim of reverse delegation, take steps immediately to send the problems back to the people who own them. The next time someone comes to see you with a problem, make sure he takes the monkey with him when he leaves. You'll both be better off for this decision.

14

Getting

Started

Effective team time management is not easy. It requires changing habits, and that means lots of hard work. You can't simply command it to take place. So, what is the key? How do you make it happen? Peter Drucker, one of our favorite management seers, offers this insight: "One thing is clear . . . [teamwork] will require greater self-discipline and even greater emphasis on individual responsibility for relationships and for communication."*

Who is responsible for team time management? We all are! What's the key to making it happen? Self-discipline! Discipline is the special ingredient that makes anything possible. It means doing what we know we should do, whether we feel like it or not. Team time management is based on decisions, not feelings. Self-discipline means following through on your decisions.

Since the 1960s, many people have considered discipline a negative idea. The mood was long one of impulse and spontaneity. We did what felt good. Discipline connoted rigidity and

---

*Peter Drucker, "The Coming of the New Organization," *Harvard Business Review*, January–February 1988, p. 47.

coercion; it seemed opposed to the freedom we all wanted so desperately—freedom to be and to do only what we wanted to do, what we felt like doing.

But we found that, with no rules and few guidelines, we went nowhere. Without direction, we ended up running around in circles. No matter how fast we ran, we never seemed to get any nearer to our goals.

Discipline is actually a positive idea. Discipline is forming the right habits that make our lives, day by day, a success instead of a failure. It is the routine that carries us through the hard times which come with greater and greater responsibility. It is, as much as possible, learning to *want* to do what we have to do in order to succeed.

Not only does it take discipline to create effective team time management, it takes discipline to overcome our own insecurities. A disciplined mind learns to sort out the difference between what is real and what is only perceived. Discipline conquers the negative attitudes that invade our minds. Discipline allows us more control over the clock.

Discipline is the difference between success and failure. Earl Nightingale has said that the secret of success is simply that successful people form the habit of doing what failures don't want to do.* What are these things? They are the very things that none of us, successes or failures, really like to do. Yet successful people do them anyway.

For example, successful team players accept the responsibility for effective communication and take the time necessary to make sure it takes place. Failures assume it's up to the other person to get it. Successes take time to plan and coordinate everything. Failures complain that they don't have enough time. Successes work at improving team processes, whereas failures just keep on doing what they've always done.

Successful team members do these things because they know that by doing them they can achieve their goals. In other words, they do these things because they like the results they obtain. Failures, by contrast, tend to accept whatever results

*Earl Nightingale, *The Strangest Secret*, cassette tape (Chicago: Nightingale-Conant Corporation, 1972).

they get by doing only the things they like to do. Self-discipline produces better habits, which bring about better results.

The changes required of everyone involved in teams may look somewhat frightening at first because change almost always causes apprehension. However, a quick look at what many are leaving behind is an encouragement to work harder at the team time management approach. Working alone in a superior/subordinate mode often:

- Breeds confusion and a lack of trust.
- Fosters the feeling of not being listened to.
- Encourages bureaucratic office politics.
- Minimizes any chance of working on bigger issues.
- Confuses everyone concerning the quality of their work.
- Involves arbitrary rules and regulations.
- Permits a boss to take credit for someone else's ideas.
- Limits resources for doing a job well.
- Simplifies a job to the point of rendering it meaningless.
- Encourages superiors to treat subordinates like interchangeable parts.

Most of us can readily identify with at least some of these negative characteristics of the old work mode. They do not foster the favorable environment we must have to achieve the results we so desperately need. We have only to compare this list with the list of possibilities offered by team time management to envision the direction we must take. Working with team time management usually:

- Encourages trust and responsibility.
- Mandates that everyone's ideas be listened to.
- Allows various team members to solve problems as a team.
- Acknowledges the importance of each person and provides an environment of encouragement, support, and approval.
- Demands clarity of goals, directions, and measurable results.
- Provides feedback.

- Develops two-way communication as part of the structure.
- Allows for the best allocation of time for all involved.
- Sees morale, interpersonal skills, and productivity improve at a rapid rate.

There is no contest here. It's an obvious choice between positive influences and negative ones. Strong working teams are successful; threatening superior/subordinate concepts lead only to failure. As the old saying goes, "You cannot direct the wind, but you can adjust the set of the sail." It's time that we set sail for a way that works instead of continually fighting choppy waters. It's time we sailed as a united crew instead of all of us moving individually in different directions.

Training and Developing Everyone

Soichiro Honda, the late president of Honda Motors, once criticized American business for being overly concerned with its "A" people—the superstars. Americans, he claimed, spent a lot of time and money on their development, but acted as though only the home-run hitters were important, quickly losing interest in those who couldn't or didn't hit home runs. By contrast, he said, Japanese businesses were as concerned with the "B, C, D, E, F, and G" people as they were with the "A" people. A company is ultimately no better than its worst employees, he concluded.

That's something worth thinking about. We've noticed that companies are quick to provide time management training for managers, but slow to provide the same training for others. We're often told that it costs too much. The result is that managers are the most trained group in America, while administrative staff people are the least trained group.

Training is closely linked to expectations. If we don't expect much from some group or level of employees, we won't spend much time or money on training them. But expectations are also closely linked to performance. People tend to live up—or down—to what is expected of them. If poor performance is expected, poor performance will be delivered. If great accomplishments are called for, these too will be delivered. Learn to have faith in and respect for your employees; you will be the winner and so will they. Expect a lot, get a lot; expect little, and get little. This is the Pygmalion effect and the self-fulfilling prophecy at work.

The more faith in and respect for employees we have, the more time and money we will devote to training and developing them. The more they feel important because of the time and attention they receive, the more they will try to improve. The more we train them, the more they will deliver. Everyone wins.

Training and developing people requires a tremendous amount of time. Unfortunately, many managers let training and development slide to the end of the line, then try to improve performance by exhorting people to adopt good time management principles. Time teamwork can thrive only when people feel motivated to be team players.

Extending team time concepts to everyone should be part of your regular training and development effort. To develop others, you must understand time management concepts, use them, be committed to the goal of development, and actively make time for it. You must have your own time in control before you can hope to influence others. If you do one thing and say another, others are more likely to follow the example of your actions, not your words.

Promoting Team Time Management

We've now presented you with all the arguments in favor of team time management and shown you in detail how it works and how it will benefit you. Making a success of the concept involves remembering these twenty-five "musts."

1. Commit yourself to being part of the team, not just its leader.
2. Emphasize cooperation, not competition. To get more teamwork, reward teamwork.

3. Remember that managers exist to facilitate performance. Subordinates are not here to serve superiors; superiors are here to serve subordinates.
4. Try to think of others at least as often as you think of yourself.
5. Learn to see people's strengths rather than their weaknesses. Help them to accentuate and build on these strengths.
6. Approach time from a team standpoint, remembering that different people perceive time differently. Develop an ongoing dialogue on how best to use team time.
7. Take time to communicate effectively. This involves being a good listener as well as a good talker. Good communication saves time in the long run and prevents many problems.
8. When instructing others, be sure you provide complete information and clear instructions. Check to be sure your teammates really understand everything.
9. Improve your methods for planning and coordinating projects and activities.
10. Start earlier. Ask for things before they're due. Allow more lead time. Give people plenty of advance notice.
11. Make sure your expectations are reasonable.
12. Discuss objectives, priorities, and plans with others. Do it often.
13. Make sure everyone is always well informed.
14. Set aside regular time slots for talking with key people. Don't just drop in on them spontaneously.
15. Analyze everything you do and look for ways to improve each facet of the operation. Ask team members for ideas on how to improve everything. The more ideas you collect, the more likely you are to improve.
16. Look for ways to save time for the people you work with. Ask others how you waste their time and act on their suggestions.
17. Make sure your meetings are productive. Don't meet without a clear purpose. Follow an agenda and be sure to follow up.

18. Develop the on-time habit. Show up for meetings and appointments on time, deliver work on time, make sure that others never have to wait for you, and encourage others to do the same.
19. Don't interrupt others any more than you have to. Bunching items you must discuss cuts down on interruptions. Get team members to follow the same policy.
20. Establish a quiet-time policy for your company or office. Help people to concentrate on their work by freeing them from unnecessary distractions.
21. Make time to train and coach everyone.
22. Develop an excellent working relationship with your secretary.
23. Learn to be an effective delegator.
24. Don't wait for someone else to take the initiative in developing a strong support team to help everyone achieve more. Assume that the team's success depends on you. "If it is to be, it is up to me."
25. Practice the Golden Rule: Treat other people the way you would like to be treated. Show appreciation, and help your team by being more generous with your praise than with your criticism.

New Habits, New Heart

Ultimately, to be successful—in team time management or in anything else—you must act. Success demands two things: You must know what to do, and you must do it. There is a big difference between the two. As Will Rogers used to say, "It may be common sense, but that doesn't mean it's common practice." Throughout this book, we've been discussing know-how. All you need now is the commitment and discipline to act.

To make team time management work, you need new habits. The key to changing your habits is a change in heart. You've got to want to. In Chapter 1, we argued that individualism must be balanced with "teamism." To do this, you must adjust your thoughts, your beliefs, your attitudes.

To get your heart change started, you might ponder this advice from one of history's great team builders:

1. Develop a spirit of unity. Concentrate on your common purpose.
2. Remember that we're all like parts of a body, and it takes every one of us to make it complete, even though we each have different work to do.
3. Be kind, compassionate, and forgiving with each other.
4. When you make decisions, be sure to consider the interests of everyone involved, not just your own. In fact, you should put others' interests ahead of your own.

We believe this advice, given by St. Paul to the early Christian church over 1,900 years ago,* is also valid advice for organizations today. Those who follow this advice will build strong, effective teams that make good use of everyone's time.

Nothing is lost until you begin looking for it. You may not realize how much you're missing until you become aware of all that positive team time management can do for you. Once you know, however, you must begin looking for it, you must begin trying to promote good team time management. The effort is worth it because the results are so great.

*See Rom. 12:4–5, Eph. 4:32, Phil. 2:2–4.

Index